Contents

5 Islamic Thought in the Modern World 82

6 Looking to the Future 98

Foreword

Religions of the World

The informed citizen or student needs a good overall knowledge of our small but complicated world. Fifty years ago you might have neglected religions. Now, however, we are shrewder and can see that religions and ideologies not only form civilizations but directly influence international events. These brief books provide succinct, balanced, and informative guides to the major faiths and one volume also introduces the changing religious scene as we enter the new millennium.

Today we want not only to be informed, but to be stimulated by the life and beliefs of the diverse and often complex religions of today's world. These insightful and accessible introductions allow you to explore the riches of each tradition—to understand its history, its beliefs and practices, and also to grasp its influence upon the modern world. The books have been written by a team of excellent and, on the whole, younger scholars who represent a new generation of writers in the field of religious studies. While aware of the political and historical influences of religion these authors aim to present the religion's spiritual side in a fresh and interesting way. So whether you are interested simply in descriptive knowledge of a faith, or in exploring its spiritual message, you will find these introductions invaluable.

The emphasis in these books is on the modern period, because every religious tradition has transformed itself in the face of the traumatic experiences of the last two hundred years or more. Colonialism, industrialization, nationalism, revivals of religion, new religions, world wars, revolutions, and social transformations have not left faith unaffected and have drawn on religious and anti-religious forces to reshape our world. Modern technology in the last 25 years—from the Boeing 747 to the world wide web—has made our globe seem a much smaller place. Even the moon's magic has been captured by technology.

We meet in these books people of the modern period as a sample of the many changes over the last few centuries. At the same time, each book provides a valuable insight into the different dimensions of the religion: its teachings, narratives, organizations, rituals, and experiences. In touching on these features, each volume gives a rounded view of the tradition enabling you to understand what it means to belong to a particular faith. As the native American proverb has it: "Never judge a person without walking a mile in his moccasins."

To assist you further in your exploration, a number of useful reference aids are included. Each book contains a chronology, map, glossary, pronunciation guide, list of festivals, annotated reading list, and index. A selection of images provides examples of religious art, symbols, and contemporary practices. Focus boxes explore in more detail the relation between the faith and some aspect of the arts—whether painting, sculpture, architecture, literature, dance, or music.

I hope you will find these introductions enjoyable and illuminating. Brevity is supposed to be the soul of wit: it can also turn out to be what we need in the first instance in introducing cultural and spiritual themes.

Ninian Smart
Santa Barbara, 1998

Preface

Writing a brief introductory book of this kind presents a set of unique challenges to the author, who must balance brevity, clarity, and comprehensiveness. These demands are particularly acute in the case of Islam, which is a religion of people from vastly varying cultures, and simultaneously one perceived as foreign to the Western world. In the interest of clarity I have chosen to concentrate on a limited number of societies when providing concrete examples of Islamic beliefs and customs, and must apologize to those readers whose regional interests have not been sufficiently accommodated.

Emphasizing Islam as a living tradition, I have provided only the most condensed description of classical Islamic history and thought, subjects which are covered in great detail in a variety of books. I have tried to focus on the religion of ordinary Muslims, who live in societies that are mostly in a state of relative peace, and whose major concerns revolve around the day-to-day issues that preoccupy human beings in most societies. I have intentionally avoided the Islam of newspaper headlines; nor have I attempted to make religious sense of the madness that has gripped Afghanistan and Algeria.

I have tried to be as consistent as possible in my use of technical terms that have not been standardized in scholarly use. For example, I use "Muslim" as an adjective to refer to both men and women who profess the religion of Islam. I also use "Muslim" as an adjective referring to societal or historical phenomena that are religious in content or character. This is distinct from my use of the term "Islamic" to refer to those features of life that are shared even by the non-Muslim members of a predominantly Muslim society, such as its art or music. This formula parallels the usage of "Christian" versus "Western" in the book. I have used Arabic technical terms only where absolutely necessary, and have used a simplified system of transliteration—interested readers should consult the pronunciation guide for clarification. Arabic words that have entered the English language are treated as English words when written in plural form; singular and plural forms of other words are provided as necessary.

This book emerges from roughly ten years of teaching introductory courses on Islam, and I would like to acknowledge the contribution of students, both past and present, at Amherst, Yale, and Brown, for forcing me to think about the material in new ways. My frequent research trips to the Islamic world have been facilitated by a number of granting agencies and academic institutions, most significantly Amherst College.

In putting together this volume I have drawn information from a large number of people in the Islamic world and in the United States. Among those scholars whose direct communications I was acutely aware of during the months in which I was writing this book are Eqbal Ahmed, Leila Ahmed, Virginia Aksan, Adel Allouche, Gerhard Böwering, Amila Buturovic, Michael Cooperson, Alan Godlas, Yvonne Haddad, Farooq Hamid, Nancy Hill, Ahmet Karamustafa, Nevzat Kaya, Ahmet Kuyaş, Ali Mirsepassi, Dwight Reynolds, Ahmed Tasbihi, Shawkat M. Toorawa, E. Sarah Wolper, and Osman Yahya. There are, no doubt, many others whom I have overlooked, but neither they nor the people named above are in any way accountable for the shortcomings of this book.

I would particularly like to thank Melanie White, my editor at Calmann and King, for her patience with the delays necessitated by my schedule, Shahzad Bashir for reading the manuscript and commenting on it, and Mehrin Masud for her careful reading, for listening to me formulate ideas, and for keeping the cappuccinos coming.

Jamal J. Elias
June 1998

Chronology of Islam

c. 570 C.E.	Birth of the Prophet in Mecca.
619	Death of Khadija, first wife of the Prophet and first convert to Islam.
622	The Hijra: the emigration of Muhammad and his followers from Mecca to Medina, marking the beginning of the Islamic lunar calendar.
630	Conquest of Mecca.
632	The Farewell Pilgrimage and death of the Prophet.
632	Death of Fatima, daughter of the Prophet and wife of Ali.
632–4	Abu Bakr is Caliph.
634–44	Umar is Caliph.
635	Conquest of Damascus.
639	Conquest of Egypt.
640	Conquest of Persia.
644	Death of Umar.
644–56	Uthman is Caliph.
651	Death of the last pre-Islamic Persian emperor, Yazdigird.
653	Official date of the canonization of the Qur'an under Uthman.
656	Death of Uthman.
656–61	Ali is Caliph.
657	Battle of Siffin between supporters of Ali and the army of Mu'awiya.
661	Assassination of Ali. Mu'awiya becomes Caliph.
661–750	Umayyad dynasty.
678	Death of A'isha, wife of the Prophet and one of the most influential figures in early Islam.
680	Husayn, son of Ali and grandson of the Prophet, martyred at Karbala.
711	Conquest of Spain.
711–12	Conquest of Indus Valley.
750	Defeat of the Umayyads by the Abbasid dynasty.
762	The city of Baghdad founded as the seat of the Caliphate and capital of the Abbasids.
765	Death of Ja'far al-Sadiq, the sixth Shi'i Imam. He is the last Imam to be recognized by both the Twelver Shi'is and the Isma'ilis, and is highly regarded for his religious knowledge.
767	Death of the great legal scholar, Abu Hanifa.
784–6	Building of the Great Mosque in Cordoba, Spain.
786–809	Reign of the famous Caliph, Harun al-Rashid.
801	Death of the ascetic mystic, Rabi'a al-Adawiya.
813–33	Reign of the Abbasid Caliph al-Ma'mun, under whom there was a great flowering in Islamic scholarship and literature. Major theological debate over the nature of the Qur'an.

817	Attempt at reconciling Shi'i and Sunni Islamic sects.
820	Death of al-Shafi'i, a famous legal scholar.
855	Death of the theologian and legal scholar, Ibn Hanbal.
870	Death of Bukhari, the famous compiler of Hadith.
874	The twelfth Imam of the Twelver Shi'is, Muhammad al-Qa'im, goes into a state of concealment. He is not expected to return until the events that signal the end of this world.
875	Death of Muslim Ibn al-Hajjaj, the famous compiler of Hadith.
890	First appearance of Isma'ili religious and political insurgents in Iraq.
c. 900	Rise of Zaydi Shi'ism in Yemen.
928	Raid on Mecca and desecration of the Ka'ba by the extremist Isma'ili followers of Hamdan Qarmat.
935	Death of the great theologian, al-Ash'ari.
950	Death of the philosopher, al-Farabi.
970	Foundation of the Al-Azhar Mosque in Cairo.
1037	Death of the philosopher, Ibn Sina (known in the West as Avicenna).
1064	Death of Ibn Hazm, a theologian, philosopher, poet, and jurisprudent, and possibly the greatest scholar to come out of Islamic Spain.
1075	Battle of Manzikert, in which the Seljuk Turks defeated the Byzantine army and captured the Byzantine Emperor Romanus Diogenus, thereby opening the Byzantine territories to future invasion and conquest.
1099	Crusaders capture Jerusalem.
1111	Death of the famous theologian, Al-Ghazali.
1153	Death of Muhammad al-Shahrastani, a historian of religion famous for his *Book of Religions and Sects*.
1187	Retaking of Jerusalem from the Crusaders by Saladin.
1198	Death of the great Spanish philosopher, Ibn Rushd (known in the West as Averroes).
1220	The Mongol invasion of the Islamic world.
1240	Death of the great Spanish mystical philosopher, Ibn al-Arabi.
1258	Mongol conquest of Baghdad and the end of the Abbasid Caliphs.
1260	Battle of Ayn Jalut, at which the Egyptian Mamluks defeated the Mongols, preventing them from invading Africa.
1273	Death of the famous mystical poet, Jalal al-Din Rumi.
1453	Conquest of Byzantium (Constantinople) by the Ottoman Turks.
late 1400s	Muslim communities established in southern West Africa.
1492	The fall of Granada and the end of the last Muslim principality in Spain.
1501–24	Reign of Shah Isma'il I, a founder of the Safavid Empire in Iran.
1502	Twelver Shi'ism is made official religion of Iran.
1505	Death of Al-Suyuti, a famous Egyptian historian, grammarian, and scholar of the Qur'an.

1517	Ottoman conquest of Egypt, after which the Ottoman emperor also claims to be the Caliph of the Islamic world.
1520–66	Reign of Ottoman emperor Süleyman the Magnificent, who makes the Ottoman claim to be the main rulers of the Sunni Islamic world a reality.
1526–30	Reign of the Emperor Babur, who laid the foundations of the Mughal Empire in India.
c. 1550	Islam arrives in Cambodia.
mid 1500s	Islam becomes established in Borneo.
1550–7	Construction of the Süleymaniye Mosque in Istanbul.
1609–14	The expulsion of all Muslims from Spain.
1624	Death of the Indian mystic and reformer Ahmad Sirhindi
1744	Alliance between the religious reformer Ibn Abd al-Wahhab and Muhammad Ibn Saʿud, which eventually led to the creation of Saudi Arabia.
1792	Death of Abd al-Wahhab.
1798	Napoleon invades Egypt.
1803	Establishment of the Sokoto Caliphate in West Africa.
1817	Death of Usuman Dan Fodio, founder of the Sokoto Caliphate.
1897	Death of the reformer Jamal Ad-Din Al-Afghani.
1898	Death of the reformer Sayyid Ahmad Khan.
1906	Constitutional reform in Iran.
1917	Abolition of the Sunni caliphate.
1924	Turkey becomes the first Muslim-majority secular republic.
1939	Death of the philosopher and poet Muhammad Iqbal.
1947	Pakistan is established as the first modern republic based on religion as nationalism.
1966	Death of the Islamist reformer Sayyid Qutb.
1977	Death of the Iranian activist and religious intellectual Ali Shariʿati.
1979	Creation of the Islamic Republic of Iran under Ayatollah Khomeini.
1979	Death of the Islamist reformer and founder of the Jamaʿat-e Islami, Abu'l-Aʿla Mawdudi.
1989	Death of Ayatollah Khomeini
1991	Dissolution of the Soviet Union provides independence to Muslim-majority Soviet republics that had formerly been Russian colonies.
1992	Bosnia-Hercegovina declares its independence as the only Muslim-majority pluralistic society in Europe, and is immediately occupied by the Serbian Yugoslav People's Army, which, together with its allies, embarks on a policy of genocidal ethnic cleansing.
1998	Pakistan becomes the first Islamic country to test a nuclear weapon.

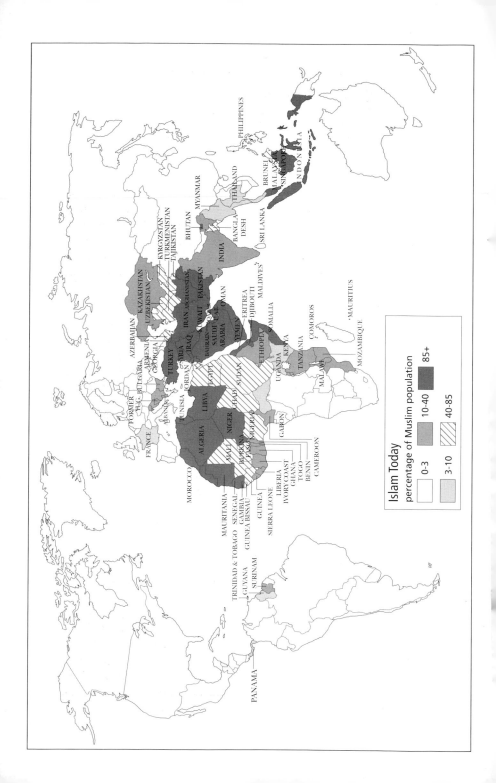

Islam Today

percentage of Muslim population

- 0–3
- 3–10
- 10–40
- 40–85
- 85+

PHILIPPINES

BRUNEI
MALAYSIA
SINGAPORE
INDONESIA

THAILAND

MYANMAR

BHUTAN

BANGLA-
DESH

SRI LANKA

INDIA

MALDIVES

MAURITIUS

KYRGYZSTAN
TURKMENISTAN
TAJIKISTAN

KAZAKHSTAN

UZBEKISTAN

AFGHANISTAN
PAKISTAN

OMAN
U.A.E.
SAUDI
ARABIA
QATAR
BAHRAIN
KUWAIT
IRAN
IRAQ

YEMEN

ERITREA
DJIBOUTI

SOMALIA

AZERBAIJAN

ARMENIA
GEORGIA

TURKEY

SYRIA
JORDAN

ETHIOPIA
KENYA

UGANDA

COMOROS

TANZANIA

MOZAMBIQUE

FORMER
U.S.S.R.

BULGARIA

ALBANIA

EGYPT
SUDAN

MALAWI

TUNISIA

LIBYA

CHAD

FRANCE

MOROCCO

ALGERIA

NIGER

NIGERIA

GABON

CAMEROON

BENIN
TOGO

BURKINA
FASO

GHANA

IVORY COAST

LIBERIA

GUINEA

SIERRA LEONE

GUINEA BISSAU

GAMBIA

SENEGAL

MAURITANIA

TRINIDAD & TOBAGO

GUYANA

SURINAM

PANAMA

Islam in Everyday Life and Society 1

There are, needless to say, numerous things that I, as a Muslim immigrant to the United States, miss about the place where I spent much of my youth. I have come to realize that the lack I have felt most deeply in my life in New England is not environmental, architectural, culinary, or social (although all such wants are there as well): it is the absence of a sound, that of the Islamic call to prayer, or *adhan* (sometimes *azan*).

One of the most distinctive features of any Muslim societal landscape is that five times a day a human voice rings out, marking the time for prayer. In most cultures the sound is musical, in parts of Africa it is consciously not so, but everywhere the Arabic words are instantly recognizable for what they are:

> God is Greatest! God is Greatest! God is Greatest! God is Greatest! I witness that there is no god but God! I witness that there is no god but God! I witness that Muhammad is the messenger of God! I witness that Muhammad is the messenger of God! Come to prayer! Come to prayer! Come to salvation! Come to salvation! God is Greatest! God is Greatest! There is no god but God!

The *adhan* is delivered shortly before the times of the five daily ritual prayers, which can be performed in a **mosque**—a building dedicated to the purpose—or, as is practiced more frequently, at home. Like members of other religious communities, the majority of Muslims are not strict observers of religious ritual and pray somewhat irregularly. But even for those Muslims who pray infrequently, the *adhan* marks the passage of time through the day (in much the same way as church bells do in many Christian communities) and serves as a constant reminder that they are living in a Muslim community. Equally importantly, the Arabic used for the *adhan* directly evokes a connection to the **Qur'an** (often rendered as "Koran" in English), the Islamic scripture that is believed by Muslims to be God's literal word, and thereby reaffirms God's continual presence in human life. The scriptural connection signified by the *adhan* was ingrained in me, while growing up, by my parents, who stopped eating and drinking when they heard the call to prayer and refrained from all idle conversation until it was over. As a child, I simultaneously respected the *adhan* for its religious significance, considered it an intrusion on my routine (for example my parents told me to stop playing music when it sounded), and learned to ignore it enough to sleep through the first one of the day, which rings out shortly before dawn. Now when I travel from my home, a charming town where not even church bells are allowed to disturb the peace, to Muslim cities for research or to visit friends and relatives, the morning *adhan* always wakes me up. It is a welcome intrusion on my routine, because I find the sound reassuring and emotionally evocative.

The Muslim World Today

Islam is a religion with approximately 1 billion adherents worldwide, with established populations on every inhabited continent of the planet. Within a hundred years of its emergence in the Arabian peninsula in the seventh century C.E., Muslim communities could be found living in Asia, Africa, and Europe. It was through Islamic centers of learning and the work of Muslim scholars that much of Greek thought reached Christian Europe. Muslim scientists made major scientific contributions, such as the algebraic system, the number zero, and elliptical orbits in astronomy. The importance of Muslims to the development of western Mediterranean culture is hinted at in some of the words of Arabic origin which continue into English (there are far more examples in Spanish and Portuguese): algebra, rice, admiral, sherbet.

A remarkable feature of Islamic history is that, with only one significant exception, all lands to which Islam spread among the population have remained Muslim into modern times. The exception is Spain and Portugal, where the long process of Christian reconquest (called the Reconquista), followed by the Spanish Inquisition, systematically eradicated the area's Muslim population. Even so, when the edict for the final expulsion of Muslims and Jews was issued in 1619 (127 years after the end of the Reconquista in 1492), around two million Muslims fled the kingdom of Castile alone, giving some indication of the degree to which Islam had been integrated into Spanish life.

Islam continues to be the majority religion in countries as diverse as Morocco in the west and Indonesia in the east, and from Senegal in the south to Kazakhstan in the north. In each of these countries Islam is practiced in a distinct way, these differences being most apparent in the way people dress and in their customs surrounding such life-events as birth and marriage. Thus Bosnian Muslims live their lives in ways that have more in common with their Christian neighbors than with the Muslims of Pakistan, and the Muslims of Indonesia have incorporated many elements of Hindu mythology into their religious lives. In other places, local Muslim customs reflect the need to set the Muslims off from their non-Muslim neighbors. For example, Indian Muslims eat particular foods and avoid certain colors and flowers in their weddings for the specific purpose of maintaining their differences from the Hindu majority. It is therefore possible to speak of numerous "fault-lines" of identity along which one can differentiate Muslims, these being lines of language, ethnicity, race, nationhood, gender, attitudes toward the modern world, experience with colonialism, age, economic status, social status, sectarian identity, and so on. Any statement about Muslim beliefs that claims to be universal inevitably ends up being disproved by exceptions somewhere in the Muslim world.

Nonetheless, the majority of Muslims retain a remarkable similarity in their rituals, a fact that is reinforced by the almost universal use of Arabic as the language of prayer and liturgy. Furthermore, even though Muslims have as highly developed a sense of nationalism and patriotism as anyone else, many of them retain the sense that they all belong to one community, or *umma*. For this reason, the Muslim citizens of a particular region or country will greet fellow Muslims from distant, unrelated societies with a warmth and sense of kinship that is very rare in most other religious communities. And even though some Muslims, particularly activists with an extremely politicized understanding of Islam, will criticize other Muslims to the point of considering them nonbelievers or apostates, when the Muslims of whom they are critical are faced with an external threat (as in Bosnia), the first group will frequently suspend its criticism and extend the umbrella of their sympathy and aid to the Muslims in need of support.

The central shared characteristic of all Muslims is their belief in a God who sent a verbal revelation called the Qur'an (or Koran) through a human prophet named **Muhammad**, who was born around 570 C.E. in the Arabian city of Mecca and died in the nearby city of Medina in 632 C.E.[1] The specific ways in which God's identity, the nature of revelation, and the concept of prophecy are understood have varied over time and in different contexts, but the centrality of these elements in defining Islamic identity has not changed.

God is commonly referred to by His Arabic name **Allah**, most likely derived from *al-ilah*, literally meaning "The God." He is also frequently called "al-Rabb," Arabic for "the Lord." He is often also referred to using whatever the generic word for God is in the various languages spoken by Muslims (for example "Khuda" in Indo-Iranian languages and "Tanri" or "Tengri" in Turkic ones). Western scholarship on Islam has sometimes represented the Muslim God as being stern and wrathful, and the relationship of human beings to Him as one of a servitude largely motivated by fear of punishment and, secondarily, the desire for sensual rewards in heaven. For many Muslims, however, the overarching characteristics of God are His nurturing mercy and compassion; the ideal attitude that human beings should have toward Him is not one of fearful obedience but of gratitude. Pious Muslims try to begin every action, from religious ritual to mundane activities such as beginning a journey to the grocery store, with the formula "In the name of God, the Compassionate, the Merciful." This phrase marks the opening of chapters in the Qur'an and has been used to start formal correspondence throughout Islamic history.

God's mercy and compassion are proven to many Muslims in everything from the wondrous complexity of the universe to the very fact of human existence. One of the most eloquent chapters of the Qur'an is entitled "The Merciful" (Chapter 55); using both rhyme and meter, it catalogs some of the wonders God has created and expresses a rhetorical amazement at the capacity of human beings to deny God's generosity:

> The Merciful! He taught the Qur'an; He created Man; He taught him an intelligent speech. The sun and the moon follow courses computed, and the stars, plants and trees bow down in adoration. The sky has He raised high, and He has set up the balance of justice in order that you may not transgress ... It is He who has spread out the earth for His creatures: Therein is fruit and date-palms, producing bunches of dates; also corn, with its husks and stalks for fodder, and sweet-smelling plants. Then which of your Lord's favors would you deny? (55: 1–13)

There are numerous other places in which the Qur'an speaks of God's mercy:

And He gives you all that you ask for, and if you were to add
up the favors of Allah, you would never be able to count
them. Indeed, human beings are given to injustice and
ingratitude.

(14:34)

In the face of God's overwhelming kindness, disobedience to God
becomes synonymous with denying His generosity, and evil is therefore
the same as ingratitude. Like the Qur'an, many Islamic theological writings see the entire universe as in a state of obedience to God's law; the
word **Islam** literally refers to this state of surrender. Human beings are
the only creations that have the capacity to disobey, and they do this by
arrogantly thinking that they are self-sufficient, not needing God's support or guidance.

A commonly repeated Islamic tradition states that God is closer to
a person than his or her jugular vein, implying that God permeates the
cosmos. Islamic systems of ritual observance assume that there is a
wakeful, attentive God who listens to and cares about each and every
one of His creations. Throughout the Islamic world, there is a certain
newsworthiness to miraculous stories of how the name of God or the
Islamic profession of faith appears in the pattern on the sides of a fish,
or how the bleat of a particular sheep sounds as if the animal is singing
the praises of God. A pigeon's coo sounds like "Him! Him!" in Arabic,
and in Pakistan, a partridge cries out "Glory be to Your creation!" These
stories bear a resemblance to ones encountered in the Christian world
(including the United States), but the Islamic ones underline the
Muslim belief that God permeates the universe and that He continues
to be intimately involved in its care and therefore in our lives.

Many Muslims see Islam as the submission to Divine law, and anything that has surrendered itself to this law as being called **Muslim**
(fem. *muslima*). Religious and pious human beings often prefer the
words *muhsin* and *mu'min*, the former term applying to someone who
does good deeds, is righteous and beneficent, and the latter to someone
who believes or has faith. The word for faith, *iman*, is closely related to
the words for safety, security, and trust, and for many Muslims having
faith automatically implies being in God's protection, secure within the
principles of guidance He has provided.

The belief in God's oneness is called *tawhid*, which not only means
divine unity but also a person's act of affirming that unity. The word for
piety (*taqwa*) also carries connotations of strength and empowerment.
Muslims see their relationship with God as an intimate one in which

God's creation of human beings is a blessing, and His laws and strictures are not an affliction but an act of grace providing guidance in this life. Many Muslims hold the belief that our life in this world is actually a test for an eternal afterlife; God has provided us with clear guidance through scripture and prophets, so if we still choose to disobey Him, we deserve whatever forms of unpleasantness await us in the hereafter.

The Qur'an

For many Muslims the Qur'an is the single greatest sign of God in the physical universe. In fact, individual verses of the Qur'an are called *ayat* (literally "signs"). The text refers to itself as "guidance for the world" and "a clear sign for those who can understand." It provides instructions on how to live one's life and acts as a source of ethical guidance for the things for which it does not provide clear instructions. It is a common Muslim belief that, as God's final revelation, the Qur'an contains the sum total of what God plans to reveal to humanity; therefore, behind the finite, literal message of the Qur'an is an infinite reservoir of divine wisdom. The word "Qur'an" is derived from the Arabic verb

A Muslim reads passages from the Qur'an in a quiet mosque. In addition to prayer, mosques are frequently used for study and contemplation.

meaning to read or to recite. "Qur'an" therefore means something like a recitation, or a collection of things to be recited. Muslims often refer to their scripture simply as the Qur'an but normally add a title that signifies respect, such as "al-Karim" (the Noble) or "al-Azim" (the Magnificent). Within the Qur'an itself, the term "al-Kitab" (the Book) is used as an alternative.

In the prophet Muhammad's opinion and that of the majority of pious believers, the Qur'anic revelations came from Heaven, where they were preserved on a "Well-guarded Tablet," a concealed supernatural book that existed in the presence of God. Muhammad did not become acquainted with the whole of the Qur'an at once but only with isolated sections of it. The Qur'an contains only a few obscure hints to how it was communicated to Muhammad. In fact, it is from later Islamic writings (including the **Hadith**—see p. 24) that we learn how Muhammad would occasionally go into trances when he received a revelation and would then recite it to those around him.

Muhammad believed that not only his prophetic mission but also the revelations of the earlier Hebrew prophets and the holy scriptures of the Jews and Christians were based on the original heavenly book, so that they coincided in part with what he himself taught. The Qur'an thus confirms what was revealed earlier: the laws which were given to Moses, the Gospel of Jesus, and other prophetic texts.

Although the stories contained in the Qur'an and the concept of revelation through a series of prophets are shared with the Hebrew Bible and the New Testament, the style of the Qur'an is more in keeping with that of the pre-Islamic Arab religious tradition of soothsayers. The text is written neither in prose nor poetry, but consists of rhymed prose, which is easier to remember than normal prose but is not as restricted in style as poetry.

The text is arranged in 114 chapters called **suras**. These are unequal in length, some being several pages while others are only a few lines. The chapters are not arranged in a way that reflects the order of revelation. In fact, they seem to be in roughly the opposite of the chronological order. They appear to be arranged by length, going from the longest to the shortest. Suras are traditionally identified by their names rather than their numbers. These names are normally distinctive or unusual words that appear somewhere in the early part of the sura, for example The Cow, The Bee, The Fig, Day Break, and The Clatterer. The suras are further subdivided into verses called *ayat*. Twenty-nine of the chapters begin with seemingly disjointed letters which are referred to as the "mysterious letters," which may convey some secret religious meaning, or may just signify a filing system for organizing the Qur'an.

The Qur'an was not put together during Muhammad's lifetime but was preserved on whatever material was then available: bits of parchment, leaves, shoulder blades of camels, and in the memory of his followers. After Muhammad's death people decided to start collecting the work, but the process took several years. Some say that the Qur'an was collected in its present form within two years of his death under the leadership of his friend and successor, **Abu Bakr** (d. 634). Others contend that the Caliph Umar (d. 644) was the first to compile the Qur'an. Vast arguments have raged ever since, concerning issues of theology and early Arab history, over who gathered together the first edition, and what it consisted of. Today, however, most agree that the established canon of the Qur'an, the written text Muslims use today, was completed between 650 and 656, during the reign of Umar's successor, the Caliph Uthman. His commission decided what was to be included and what excluded; it also fixed the number and order of the Suras. That said, unofficial versions of the Qur'an were not entirely forgotten, and these were referred to in subsequent histories and commentaries on the Qur'an.

While the promulgation of the official text of the Qur'an under Uthman was a major step toward uniformity in versions of the scripture, its importance may easily be exaggerated. For one thing, knowledge of the Qur'an among Muslims was based far more on memory than on writing. For another, the early Arabic script of the Qur'an was a sort of shorthand: only consonants were written, and the same letter shape could indicate more than one sound. This script was simply an aid to memorization; it presupposed that the reader had some familiarity with the text. It was not until the reign of Abd al-Malik (685–705) that the modern Arabic script was created, with its vowels and use of one letter shape for one sound.

The Centrality of the Qur'an in Islamic Tradition

Belief in the Qur'an being God's literal word has had far-reaching implications: there has traditionally been some resistance to the Qur'an's translation from Arabic into other languages. And although this reticence is now largely gone, traditional etiquette still requires that one refer to printed volumes of the Qur'an as *masahif* (sing. *mushaf*: literally, "binding" or "volume"), implying that the divine word is singular and cannot be perfectly contained in ink and paper. It is still uncommon for bookstores to write prices on copies of the Qur'an; the appropriate etiquette for a potential purchaser is to ask what the suitable "gift" for the volume should be.

The special status accorded to the Qur'an goes far beyond the semantics of what to call it. To this day there is great prestige in memorizing the text, and one who knows it in its entirety is called *hafiz* (literally "guardian"), an honorific title which hearkens back to a time when the Qur'an was transmitted orally and committing it to memory was to participate in guarding the text from loss or corruption. Children across the Islamic world, whether they know any Arabic or not, take Qur'an lessons in which they learn the Arabic script and how to sound the words phonetically. Pious Muslims often try to read a thirtieth of the book every night, so that they can finish the Qur'an every month. Those who cannot read simply run their fingers along its lines, believing that they derive merit through this simple act of devotion.

The Qur'an thus becomes simultaneously a source of prayer and a prayer in its own right, a guidebook for action as well as a ritual object. Devout Muslims treat volumes of the Qur'an with great reverence: they are not shelved with other books in the house but occupy a position of honor, and readers enter a state of ritual purity before touching them. It is common to have special bookstands to hold the text, and the most beautiful of these rank among the masterpieces of Islamic art. The Qur'an itself has been both an object and source of artistic expression. Ornate copies of the Qur'an provide outstanding examples of the art of bookmaking. Furthermore, calligraphy—which commonly uses as its subject words or phrases from the Qur'an—has emerged as one of the most highly developed art forms in the Islamic world. Qur'anic calligraphy is used to decorate a wide range of objects, from buildings to ceramic and metal vessels and even items of clothing.

The captivating sound of Qur'anic recitation is used to open most religious and official functions in the Islamic world, and skilled Qur'anic reciters enjoy a high status in the society. Given the importance accorded to the Qur'an it should come as no surprise that the human conduit of the text, the Prophet Muhammad, is similarly venerated. The Qur'an refers to Muhammad as a blessing from God, a messenger, a warner, a guide, the bringer of good news, and good news in and of himself. Muslims commonly believe that Muhammad was a human being like any other who was chosen by God to be the last of His prophets and to be the instrument He used to reveal the Qur'an. The Qur'an itself emphasizes the ordinariness of Muhammad, commanding him to say that he

ART FOCUS

Islamic Art

IN ADDITION TO CALLIGRAPHY and architecture, a wide variety of arts have been and continue to be practiced in the Islamic world. Textile arts, particularly woven carpets, continue to be highly valued around the world; there is also a long-standing tradition of making fine ceramics and glassware. In fact, the only visual art form that is noticeably absent in traditional Islamic cultures is sculpture, because it is considered to be too closely related to the construction of religious idols and icons. Islam is a vehemently iconophobic religion, that is, it forbids the physical depiction of God or any religious heroes in any form that might encourage people to make the icon an object of veneration. This intolerance stems from the religious situation in the Arabian peninsula at the time of Muhammad and is probably fueled by the ongoing contact between Muslims and members of other religious groups in places such as India and Nigeria, who continue to use icons as central elements in their religious lives. Not only are sculptures disapproved of, but sculptors are condemned for attempting to encroach on God's role as the sole creator.

The condemnations of sculpture often extend to include a general disapproval of all forms of representational religious art. Nevertheless, there is no lack of artwork in the Islamic world depicting plants, animals, human beings, and even supernatural creatures. Miniature paintings, generally intended to be bound in books, are to be ranked among the finest artistic works of Iran, Central Asia, India, and Turkey.

One can understand the wealth of visual Islamic art despite the commonly held Muslim ambivalence toward figural imagery by drawing a distinction between sacred art, which almost never makes use of human or animal imagery, and religious art, which includes religious subject matter but is not used in ritual contexts. A similar distinction can also be drawn between figural and representational arts: Islamic artists have frequently depicted suggestive "figural" imagery, as opposed to direct representations of specific living beings.[1]

Such distinctions become somewhat obscure in modern practice among some citizens of Iran and Turkey who display portraits of Muhammad's cousin **Ali**, the first leader of the **Shi'i** sect. This practice would be frowned upon by the majority of Muslims, but it is not too different from hanging a picture of the **Ka'ba**, the focus of the Islamic pilgrimage and therefore an object of great religious significance, on the wall. At a much more abstract level, one could argue that literature describing Muhammad's physical appearance in great detail—common in many Islamic communities and central to an entire genre of literature in praise of the Prophet—creates a

*Left half of the double frontispiece to Volume VII of the Qur'an of the
Egyptian Baybars Jashnagir, 1304–6. British Library, London.*

picture of Muhammad in the mind of a Muslim, and that this mental image
is no different from a physical image hanging on a wall. It would be safe to
assume, though, that many Muslims would find the difference between a
physical visual representation and a mental one easy to make, and would not
disapprove of the latter.

was a mortal man like everyone else and chastising him for losing confidence and feeling insecure.

Nonetheless, it stands to reason that Muhammad would have been of outstanding moral character to begin with if an omniscient and omnipotent God was planning to use him as a prophet. Furthermore, once Muhammad took on the role of God's messenger and exemplar to humanity, God would hardly let him engage in any activity that would contradict the divine message. According to this viewpoint, then, Muhammad had to be free from sin (and possibly even from the capacity to sin), and any frailties or errors he displayed were themselves consciously added to his character by God to fulfill a divine purpose. Muhammad has therefore become the model of behavior for most Muslims who try and follow his example, or *Sunna*, and collected anecdotes of his life, called hadiths, represent a scriptural source second only to the Qur'an.

Hadith and *Sunna*

The word "hadith" primarily means a communication or a narrative in general. In Islamic terms, it has the particular meaning of a record of actions or sayings of the Prophet and his companions. In the latter sense the whole body of the sacred tradition of Islam is called the "Hadith" and the formal study of it the "Science of Hadith."

Pre-Islamic Arabs considered it a virtue to follow the example of one's forefathers. But in the Islamic period one could hardly follow the example of ancestors who were not Muslim, so a new tradition, or *Sunna*, had to be found. This was the *Sunna* of Muhammad. After Muhammad's death the learned began systematically to develop the doctrine of duties and beliefs in accordance with the new conditions. After the early conquests Islam covered an enormous area, and new ideas as well as institutions were borrowed from the conquered peoples. Nevertheless, in Islam only the *Sunna* of the Prophet and the original Muslim community could supply rules of conduct for the believers. This soon led to the deliberate forgery of traditions: transmitters brought the words and actions of the Prophet into agreement with their own views and ideals. A very large portion of these sayings ascribed to Muhammad deals with legal provisions, religious obligations, issues of what is permissible and what forbidden, ritual purity, as well as with matters of etiquette and courtesy.

The majority of hadiths cannot therefore be regarded as really reliable historical accounts of the *Sunna* of the Prophet. As early as the eighth century, certain Islamic scholars became extremely concerned about the large number of forged hadiths that were floating about and devised an elaborate system whereby some idea of the accuracy of a hadith could be established. According to the Muslim view, a hadith account can only be considered believable if its chain of transmission (or **isnad**) offers an unbroken series of reliable authorities. The critical investigation of *isnads* has caused Muslim scholars to do research to ascertain the names and circumstances of the transmitters in a hadith account in order to investigate when and where they lived and which of them had been personally acquainted with one another. Scholars divide Hadith into three main categories according to their reliability: *Sahih* (sound), or those hadiths which have flawless chains of transmission and reinforce something that is widely accepted in the Islamic community; *Hasan* (beautiful), which are considered reliable but whose authenticity is not totally beyond doubt; and "weak" hadiths (*da'if*), which are suspect in terms of either their content or the chain of transmitters.

The earliest collections of Hadith, of which the best known was compiled by the respected scholar, Ibn Hanbal (d. 855), were arranged not according to their content but according to their transmitters. Later works were arranged by topic, two of which, those of al-Muslim (d. 875) and al-Bukhari (d. 870), are seen as so reliable that many **Sunnis** rank them just below the Qur'an itself as sacred texts.

What is contained in the Hadith is the *Sunna*, or tradition, of Muhammad, consisting of his actions and sayings and those things to which he gave unspoken approval. *Sunna* has come to mean the practice of the greater Muslim community, and in this capacity it is often referred to as the "living *Sunna*." In theory the concepts of *Sunna* and Hadith are separate but in practice they often coincide.

Muhammad had settled many questions posed to him not by revelation but by decisions made on a case-by-case basis, and the words and actions of the Prophet were recognized—even in his own lifetime—as worthy of imitation. It is for this reason that the *Sunna* of the Prophet was fixed in writing and became a standard of behavior alongside the Qur'an. Religious scholars tried to answer questions concerning the relation between the two of them. In the earliest Islamic community the *Sunna* appears to have been equal to the Qur'an in its authority. However, with the passage of time and conversion of non-Arab peoples to Islam the Qur'an gained a centrality as scripture that outstripped the importance given to the *Sunna*, particularly in its written form of Hadith.

In actual practice, many Muslims do not make a clear distinction between hadiths compiled by al-Bukhari or al-Muslim, and those that have been deemed fake by scholars. The result is an overall body of wisdom literature by which Muslims emphasize their high regard for Muhammad and learn lessons concerning ethics and morality which can then be applied to their everyday lives.

Veneration of Muhammad

Although at the level of religious doctrine and in the informal opinion of many Muslims the Qur'an occupies a higher and more central position in Islam than Muhammad does, the opposite often appears to be the case, particularly at the level of popular devotion. Most Muslims regard everything about Muhammad with deep veneration. Most of them find it difficult to utter his name without preceding and following it with terms of respect and devotion (the commonest in English being "Peace be upon him"). He is widely regarded as the ideal human being and is therefore the model for imitation. Emulation of Muhammad ranges from seeing him as a model in legal and ethical matters to seemingly trivial details in everyday life, such as how one brushes one's teeth, wears one's hair, or what food one eats.

Muhammad's presence in popular Islamic religious life is all-pervasive. There is a long-standing tradition of writing poems in praise of the Prophet, the most famous of which is the *Burda* (or "Mantle Poem"), composed in the thirteenth century by al-Busiri, which has been frequently copied in a number of languages. Other such poems in the large number of languages spoken by Muslims are frequently set to music, of which some, such as Qawwali from Pakistan, Rai from Algeria, and the songs of Moroccan Gnawa or Bangladeshi Bauls, have enjoyed considerable commercial success in the West.

Devotion to the Prophet extends to veneration of his relics. There are several shrines around the world devoted to an individual hair from his beard. When the hair vanished briefly from one such shrine in Kashmir, distraught Muslims interpreted it as an attack against Islam by the Hindu-majority Indian government and took to the streets in rioting. The emotional outbursts of some pilgrims to Muhammad's tomb in the city of Medina can be truly moving, as can the visible devotion of visitors to the reliquary in the Topkapi Palace in Istanbul, which holds the

Prophet's mantle, hairs from his beard, and a casting of what is alleged to have been a footprint he left in some mud.

Some Muslims, such as the Wahhabis of Saudi Arabia, feel extremely uncomfortable with this level of devotion to the Prophet's person, and believe that it borders on heresy by exalting Muhammad to a quasi-divine level. There is, however, no clear boundary between those who exalt Muhammad to superhuman status and those who would consider him just another human being. The real points of contention are over veneration of his physical relics, which smacks of idolatry to critics, and over his role as someone who stands between human beings and God and therefore has the power to intercede on the part of his devotees.

A frequently mentioned characteristic of Islam as a religion is the value placed upon the direct link between individual human beings and God. The so-called orthodox tradition of the legal scholars and theologians does not recognize the existence of a clergy in Islam, nor of any form of sainthood in which living or dead persons can intercede for other human beings. Yet many Muslims firmly believe in the possibility of intercession, not just by Muhammad, but also by a variety of other saintly figures including members of Muhammad's family, prominent mystical figures or Sufis, and other individuals with whom miracles are associated or who are known to be uncommonly pious. The possibility of intercession is brought up in one of the most famous verses of the Qur'an: "Who is it that can intercede before Him except as He permits?" (2:255).

The issue of intercession is a major one throughout Islam and involves questions not just of theology and the interpretation of scripture but also issues of class, culture, gender, and level of education. The acknowledgment of the possibility of intercession before God allows for the existence of saints and a clergy, and for a wide variety of religious expression. It is one of the major fault-lines along which one can divide the varieties of Muslim religious experience.

The Birth of Islam 2

Islam's historical origins lie in the life of a man named Muhammad who was born in the city of Mecca in present-day Saudi Arabia in around 570 C.E., and died in a nearby city called Medina in 632 C.E. In Muhammad's time, Arabia was culturally, politically, and economically impoverished relative to the large and wealthy empires that surrounded it. To the north were the Byzantine Greek and Sassanian Persian Empires and to the south the affluent world of Abyssinia.

Arabia itself was divided between the main Arabian plateau and a region called South Arabia (present-day Yemen), which had once been the seat of a thriving agricultural society but had fallen on poorer times. The plateau, where Muhammad was from, was an arid place in which the majority of people lived as nomads, accompanying their herds of camels, sheep, and goats from one place to another in search of good pasture. The few cities were located on oases, which provided the only reliable source of water for agriculture, and some were centers for trade among the people of Arabia and with the surrounding lands.

The Arabs of Muhammad's time lived in tribes which were large social groups held together by a shared ancestry, each being composed of a number of clans made up of several extended families. A family elder would be recognized as the leader of the clan, and the clan leaders together constituted the ruling council of a tribe. Tribal councils tried to operate through negotiation and consensus building, although powerful clans no doubt had much greater influence over tribal affairs than did weaker ones. The majority of tribes in Arabia were both patriarchal and patrineal; however, there appear to have been some tribes in which lineage was passed down through the mother, and even in very patriarchal tribes it was not uncommon for women to hold property. A good example of this was Muhammad's first wife, **Khadija**, who was a wealthy widow actively engaged in trade.

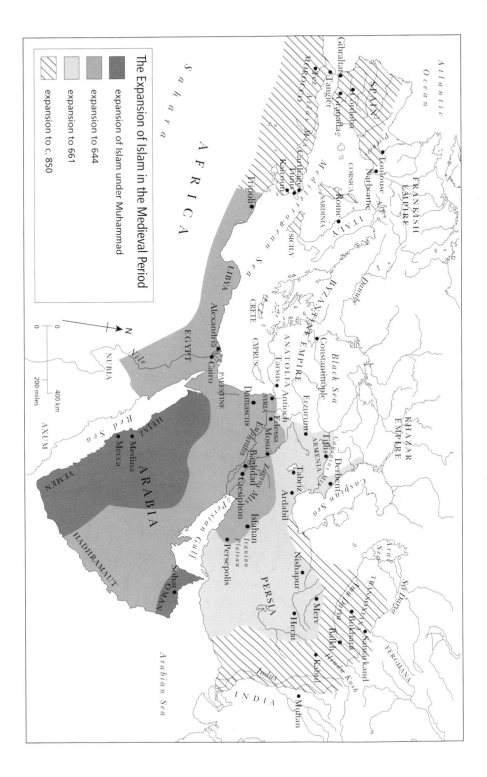

The Expansion of Islam in the Medieval Period

expansion of Islam under Muhammad

expansion to 644

expansion to 661

expansion to c. 850

The Arabian peninsula had no central government or state, but existed in a state of balance between tribes on the one hand, and the mercantile and agrarian cities on the other. Nomads who belonged to the same or allied tribes as town-dwellers would often agree not to attack these places, or the caravans going to or from them. Arabia was located at the crossroads of many trade routes; goods brought by ship to Arabian ports were loaded onto camel caravans to be transported across the desert to distant markets. Mercantile cities were heavily dependent upon the east–west trade between the Indian Ocean and the Mediterranean, and on the north–south trade between Africa and the Byzantine and Sassanian empires. Many nomadic tribes supported themselves by raiding caravans, so much so that the practice was considered an acceptable way of life and was covered by a code of conduct.

Very little is known about the religious situation in Arabia at the time of Muhammad's birth. The surrounding empires had large Christian populations, Abyssinia and the Byzantine Empire both being Christian kingdoms. Sassanian Persia (modern Iran) was officially Zoroastrian, a major religion of that time which survives today in very small numbers. Even so, Persia had a large Christian population. In addition, all the empires had significant Jewish populations. There were clearly some Christians within Arabia, but their numbers appear to have been quite small and they were individual believers, not entire clans or tribes who regarded themselves as Christian. There was also no Church based within Arabia. The number of Arabian Jews appears to have been much larger; there were entirely Jewish tribes, some of which seem to have moved to Arabia from Palestine after the destruction of the temple in Jerusalem by the Romans at the end of the first century C.E. There were probably many who, though not formally Jews, identified themselves as Israelites and were familiar with the stories of the Hebrew prophets.

The majority of Arabs did not belong to any formal religion but believed in a combination of supernatural forces, some of which they identified as spirits and others as gods. The spirits were believed to inhabit natural objects such as rocks and trees and to have influence over human lives, whereas the gods were often identified with natural phenomena such as the sun, moon, and rain. Many Arabs viewed the god of the moon and traveling, named Allah (literally, "The God"), as the ancestor and leader of the others, of which the goddesses al-Lat and Man'at also inspired popular religious cults.

The pre-Islamic Arabs did not have a detailed moral and ethical code of the kind that was developed in Islamic, Christian, and Jewish theology, nor did they commonly believe in life after death. Instead, they were governed by rules of honor, courage, and hospitality. In the absence of a belief in the afterlife, the primary way to attain immortality was to live heroic lives full of extravagant acts of valor and generosity, which were then rendered into verse by tribal poets. The Arabs were in awe of the power of poetry and poets, and viewed them as supernaturally possessed figures to be both feared and revered, not only as artists but also as tribal historians.

In addition to poets, two other figures carried great respect in pre-Islamic Arab society. The first was the soothsayer, who would foretell the future and attempt to solve problems as diverse as those of curing infertility and finding lost animals. The other was the judge, whose job it was to intercede in conflicts within a tribe and, more importantly, between tribes, as a way of avoiding violence. All these offices hold relevance for early Islamic history because, during his career as a prophet, Muhammad displayed qualities of all three, enabling his critics to label him as a poet or soothsayer in order to dismiss his religious claims.

Muhammad's Birth and Early Life

It was into this environment that Muhammad was born. His family belonged to the clan of **Hashim** in the tribe of **Quraysh** (meaning "shark"), an important merchant tribe with considerable influence in Mecca and the surrounding area. The Hashim clan, though not the most powerful in the tribe, was considered respectable. Mecca was home to a major shrine, called the Ka'ba, which was one of the few religious sites revered by people from all over Arabia. In their status as custodians of this site, the Quraysh not only gained financially from the pilgrimage business but also in reputation, because of their exclusive control of the associated rituals. Several of these were later incorporated into the **Hajj** pilgrimage, which became a central rite in Islam.

Muhammad's father, **Abdallah**, died shortly before he was born and his paternal guardianship was taken over by his grandfather, **Abd al-Muttalib**. When he was born, his mother, **Amina**, named him Ahmad while his grandfather named him Muhammad. The latter name became more common, although even to this day he is sometimes referred to as Ahmad.

Very little is known about Muhammad's childhood or about the period of his life before his career as a prophet began. The few things that we can consider to be factually true have been embellished by pious biographers who inserted real or imagined events into his early life in order to show that Muhammad was marked for greatness from the time of his birth. As a very young child Muhammad was sent to the desert to live with a nomadic tribe, a Meccan custom which perhaps derived from the desire to get children out of the unhygienic environment of the city, as well as from the belief that the nomads led a culturally "purer" Arab life. Muhammad lived with a foster family as a shepherd, and he retained a great deal of affection for them in later life, particularly for his foster mother, Halima. According to a popular legend, one day while Muhammad was herding sheep he was visited by two angels who laid him down and opened up his chest. They then took out his heart and washed it in a golden basin filled with snow before replacing it and closing him up, which probably symbolizes the removal of all existing sin from his body. However, neither the notion of primordial sin nor the belief that one can inherit one's parents' sins is prevalent in Islam.

Following this visitation, Muhammad's foster family began to fear for his safety and decided to return him to his mother before something bad happened to him. Shortly after his return to Mecca, both Muhammad's mother and grandfather died, and his guardianship was assumed by his paternal uncle, **Abu Talib**, a merchant who frequently traveled throughout Arabia. Muhammad accompanied his uncle on these expeditions, probably including one journey to Syria, and in the process not only learned the merchant's trade but also came in contact with a wide variety of people.

Upon reaching adulthood, Muhammad became a merchant himself and quickly gained a reputation for honesty and trustworthiness. A wealthy widow named Khadija noticed him and extended to Muhammad a marriage proposal, which he accepted. At the time of their wedding Muhammad was twenty-five years old and Khadija was forty. In later life Muhammad spoke fondly of the years he had spent with Khadija, who was the mother of the only children Muhammad had who survived past infancy.

In his adult years, Muhammad had developed the habit of retiring to a cave outside Mecca to meditate in private. On one such occasion he fell asleep, only to be awakened by an angelic being who commanded him "Recite!" Muhammad replied by asking what he should recite, at which the angel only repeated his initial command. After the third time the angel commanded:

> Recite! In the name of your Lord Who created.
> Created man from a clot!

Recite! And your Lord is Most Bountiful—
He taught by the pen—
Taught man that which he knew not!

(Qur'an, 96:1-5)

This event occurred when Muhammad was forty years old, and for the remainder of his life he continued to receive revelations, sometimes through the efforts of that angelic being whom he was to identify as Gabriel, and at others directly from God.

Initially Muhammad sought comfort from his wife Khadija, but over time, she convinced him to listen to the angel. Muhammad was convinced that he had been chosen as a prophet of God to bring a divine message to humankind about the existence of a unique, all-powerful God, a warning of an impending doomsday and judgment, and an encouragement to live a virtuous life.

The Great Emigration: The Hijra

At first Muhammad's preaching was met with tolerance and curiosity, but as he started to gain converts the leaders of Mecca began to perceive him as a threat and to persecute his followers. The majority of Muhammad's early followers were women, slaves, and the very poor, all of whom were extremely vulnerable to their powerful oppressors. Fearing for their safety in Mecca, Muhammad and his followers began to search for a new place to live. It so happened that a nearby town, Yathrib, needed an impartial judge to arbitrate between two powerful tribes, and they extended Muhammad an invitation to move to Yathrib and adjudicate. Muhammad agreed to do so only if certain conditions were fulfilled: (i) that his family and followers could move with him; (ii) that they would be supported until they could find means of livelihood for themselves; and (iii) that they were to be considered full citizens of the city, so that if the Meccans and their allies chose to attack the Muslims, all the citizens of Yathrib would fight on the side of the Muslims. The delegation from Yathrib agreed to these terms and a secret migration of Muslims from Mecca to this city began. Finally when all but two of Muhammad's followers (his friend Abu Bakr and his cousin Ali) had reached Yathrib, he decided to move there himself. By this time some of his opponents had realized that he represented a grave threat to their interests and had formed a pact to kill him. Hearing of their plan, Muhammad secretly left Mecca in the company of his closest friend and advisor, Abu Bakr, leaving Ali in his house. Ali was the son of Muhammad's uncle Abu Talib, and had come to live with Muhammad as his adopted son, married his daughter Fatima, and became one of the most important and influential people in the formative period of Islam.

That night Muhammad's enemies surrounded his house. Ali served as a decoy by sleeping in Muhammad's bed. When the Meccans finally broke into Muhammad's house and found Ali, they realized that Muhammad had slipped away and sent a search party to hunt him down. Legend has it that Muhammad and Abu Bakr hid in a cave to escape their pursuers, and that a spider wove a web covering the entrance to the cave. Seeing the spider web, the Meccans thought that no one had been inside in a while and turned away. After the search party had returned empty-handed, Muhammad and Abu Bakr made their way to Yathrib, and Ali followed as soon as he had settled all of Muhammad's financial and social obligations in Mecca.

The emigration of Muhammad and the Muslims from Mecca to Yathrib, which occurred in 622, marks the most important date in Islamic history. It is called the **Hijra**, or "Great Emigration"; the Muslims who emigrated are referred to as Muhajirs and those who helped them as Ansar. Great honor is attached to both groups, and throughout Islamic history, any event in which a number of Muslims have had to flee from persecution to a safe haven is seen as a repetition of the Hijra. The Hijra also marks the start of the Islamic calendar, which is used for all religious events and is the official calendar in many countries to this day.

The Hijra signals the beginning of Islam as a social religion. In Mecca Muhammad was mostly a warner and prophet bringing a message of monotheism (belief in one God) and urging people to repent of their immoral ways. In Yathrib the religion began to evolve into a social phenomenon and developed a history and complex set of laws. The city was even renamed Madinat an-nabi ("City of the Prophet"), Medina for short. While at Medina, the revelations that Muhammad received began to emphasize social laws and a sense of history, which showed Muhammad and his religion to be a continuation of the sacred tradition of the Hebrew prophets. Muhammad rapidly rose from the status of a simple prophet to that of the social, religious, and political leader of an entire community. As such, he resembled religious figures such as Moses, David, and Solomon much more than he did Jesus or the Buddha.

The Meccans perceived the Muslim community of Medina as a growing threat and engaged in three battles with them, each of which resulted in Muhammad's cause becoming much stronger. Finally in 630

C.E. the city of Mecca surrendered to Muhammad and he entered it, guaranteeing the life and property of its citizens. The only major events were the executions of a few poets who had ridiculed Muhammad and his religion, and the removal of all religious objects from the Ka'ba. Muhammad performed a pilgrimage to the Ka'ba and then returned to Medina, which he now considered his home. He made one more journey to Mecca before his death; referred to as the "Farewell Pilgrimage" it still serves as the model for one of the most important Islamic rituals, the Hajj.

Shortly after his return from the Farewell Pilgrimage, Muhammad fell gravely ill and confined himself to the house of his wife A'isha whom he had married in Mecca several years after Khadija's death. He died in her bed around midday on June 8, 632 C.E. According to a tradition which states that prophets should be buried where they die, Muhammad was buried in A'isha's chamber. Later on it was converted into a shrine and serves as an important pilgrimage site to this day.

The Islamic Community after Muhammad

Muhammad died without appointing a definite successor. Although it was very clear that there would be no prophets after him, no one was sure what the role of the next leader should be. The elders of the Islamic community decided that Muhammad's closest male companion, Abu Bakr, who was also one of the earliest converts to Islam, should lead the community after his death. Abu Bakr died only two years after Muhammad and was succeeded by another respected companion of Muhammad named Umar. It was during Umar's ten-year leadership and the twelve years of his successor, Uthman, that the Islamic community spread out of Arabia and expanded from the Mediterranean shores of North Africa to the Central Asian steppes. It was also during their time that the revelations received by Muhammad were organized into the Qur'an.

The leaders of the Islamic community after Muhammad were neither prophets nor kings. Instead, they were known as **Caliphs** (khalifa in Arabic), a word which means "representative" or "delegate," implying that they did not rule on their own authority but only as the representatives of God and His Prophet. After Uthman's death there was some confusion as to who should be the next Caliph. Many people felt that the honor should go to Muhammad's cousin and son-in-law, Ali. Others, however, favored Uthman's cousin Mu'awiya. Encouraged by their respective supporters, both men were declared Caliph and a civil war ensued. In the course of the dispute Ali was murdered by an assassin and Muʿawiya successfully seized power for himself and his family, laying the foundations of the first Islamic dynasty, known as the **Umayyads** (a reference to Muʿawiya's tribe). The majority of pious Muslims today believe that with the rise of the Umayyad dynasty the pristine institution of the Caliphate came to an end; they consider the first four Caliphs as truly virtuous, as a result of which those four are referred to as "Rightly-Guided." Even so, it was under the 100-year rule of the Umayyads that most of the lands that are still identified with Islam were conquered, and the Islamic empire extended from Spain to Pakistan.

Even though the Umayyads were in almost complete control, the dispute between the supporters of Ali and the Umayyads did not end. It took an even more serious turn when Ali's son **Husayn** and many of his family members were massacred by troops loyal to Muʿawiya's son, Yazid, in 680 C.E.

Disillusioned by the political conflict, many Muslims withdrew into a quietistic contemplation of their faith. Others devoted themselves to preaching among the citizens of the newly conquered lands, while still others dedicated their lives to the study of the Qur'an and the traditions of Muhammad and his companions. It was primarily through the efforts of such people that the Islamic world developed a rich and vibrant tradition of theology and philosophy and that the citizens of very diverse lands converted to the new religion.

Nevertheless, the succession struggles following Muhammad's death served as the primary catalysts for the initial sectarian schism within Islam, one that persists to this day. One faction maintained that Ali should have been the rightful leader of the Islamic community, and is known as the Shiʿat Ali ("Faction of Ali") or Shiʿis for short (this is the same word as **Shiʿah** and **Shiʿite**). The Shiʿi position sees the first three Caliphs as usurpers, who deprived Ali of his birthright. This belief is supported by many hadiths according to which, in his absence, Muhammad used to designate Ali as the temporary leader of the Islamic community. The most famous of these is known as the Hadith of Ghadir Khum, named after an oasis between Mecca and Medina. According to this tradition, on his return from his final visit to Mecca, Muhammad clasped Ali's hand in his and declared before the assembled crowd: "For whomever I have been a protector (*mawla*), Ali is his protector."

The implications of this hadith ride on the multiple meanings of the word *mawla*. Scholars of the Sunni sect—many of whom consider this hadith reliable since it appears in the compendium of the great Sunni scholar Ibn Hanbal with no less than ten variant readings—have taken it to mean protector or leader in a very narrow sense, implying that Ali was to be an authority only in very specific contexts. The Shi'is see it as a public declaration by Muhammad that community leadership should remain forever in the hands of the *ahl al-bayt* ("members of the household"). Few other hadiths support the Shi'i assertion, although they claim this is because the record was falsified by the supporters of Abu Bakr and later by the Umayyads. The Shi'is have their own collections of hadiths that contradict the Sunni view of events, the most important being the *Nahj al-balagha*, which is comprised of sayings and sermons attributed to Ali. Several accounts within the work provide insight into the Shi'i position regarding leadership after Muhammad:

> The family members of the Prophet (on him be blessings and peace) are the locus of divine mystery; they are where His commandments are guarded and the repositories of His knowledge, refuges for His wisdom, sanctuaries for His books, and mountain strongholds for His religion. Through them did He straighten the bowing of [the religion's] back, and through them did He banish the trembling of its flesh.[1]

A particularly eloquent reading of the events that led to the political marginalization of Ali and the Prophet's household is found in Ali's *al-Khutba al-shaqshaqiya* or "Braying Sermon." It is so named because Ali was interrupted while speaking and refused to continue it, stating that the sermon had been extemporaneous like the braying of a camel, which starts spontaneously and stops in the same way.[2] According to this account, while the family of the Prophet had been busy with his burial, Abu Bakr had usurped power for himself without consulting Ali or any of Muhammad's other close relatives. On his death, Abu Bakr had nominated his ally Umar to be the leader of the Islamic community even though this form of successorship was in complete violation of Muhammad's wishes. On Umar's death a council was convened to name a successor; it included Ali but was unfairly packed with supporters of Uthman. This ushered in a particularly dark period of oppression and nepotism which the virtuous members of the Islamic community could do little more than bear in silence.

Ali's silence in the face of these unjust transfers of power is explained by his desire to prevent bloodshed and division within the young Islamic community. However, when Uthman passed leadership to his profligate cousin Muʿawiya, Ali was forced to intervene at the behest of virtuous members of the community, who repeatedly pleaded with him to deliver them from Muʿawiya's tyrannical rule.

Sunni historians and theologians interpret the events somewhat differently. They see Abu Bakr as having been reluctant to assume leadership, and to have done so for the express purpose of holding the Islamic community together as it weathered the crisis presented by the death of its prophet. That he was the best person to assume this role was evident from his seniority in age and closeness to Muhammad. His selection of Umar as his successor was founded on a similar closeness to the Prophet and seniority as a convert. The Sunnis do not deny Ali's seniority as an early convert or his reputation for religious knowledge or zeal in service to Islam. They do, however, traditionally maintain that Ali was too young at the time of Muhammad's and Abu Bakr's deaths to become the leader of the community. In so doing, they consciously deny the kinship-based claim to leadership (which is so central to the Shiʿi view), seeing it as antithetical to Islamic teachings. There is a degree of arbitrariness to this assertion, because Abu Bakr, Umar, and Uthman were all related to Muhammad through marriage (as was Muʿawiya's father, Abu Sufyan, who was blind at the time of Uthman's death and therefore considered unfit for leadership). The strength of the Sunni position lies in the claim that it was preferable to accept a less than ideal leader than to risk the destruction of the Muslim community through civil war. In fact the name of the sect derives from the word *Sunna* (tradition) and is actually an abbreviation for a much longer term meaning "The People of Tradition (*Sunna*) and the Community," which implies a commitment to political quietism and a desire to avoid splitting into factions at whatever cost.

At most times in history the Sunni sect has taken a very inclusive attitude and tried to count as many Muslims as it could within the Sunni umbrella, even when it meant that the notion of acceptable Sunni belief had to be expanded. At the same time, being a Sunni does not necessarily imply that one agrees with the way the Sunni Islamic world is being governed, simply that one believes that it is more important to keep the Muslim community safe than it is to fight a bad ruler. Sunnis do, however, harbor some antipathy toward the Shiʿis for the disrespect they show toward figures who are highly venerated in Sunni circles. Indeed, members of some Shiʿi sects continue to ritualistically curse Abu Bakr, Umar, and Uthman, and a holiday known as *Umar-kushi* ("Umar killing") was commemorated in southwestern Iran until the middle of the twentieth century to celebrate the murder of Umar. As part of the festivities people made miniature effigies of Umar in the form of hollow cakes filled with pomegranate syrup which were stabbed, cut up, and consumed. Such practices have relied on communal segregation for their survival, and as Shi'i and Sunni societies are drawn closer together through developing global infrastructures and shared national interests, conciliatory leaders on both sides try their best to minimize their differences in belief and practice. Nonetheless, anti-Shi'i discrimination is rampant in Saudi Arabia, where the sizable Shi'i minority is all but excluded from public life, and sectarian differences play a major factor in the civil violence in Karachi and other cities in Pakistan.

In recent times, Shi'ism has developed a negative reputation for a perceived propensity toward violence, as evidenced by events in Iran following the Islamic Revolution of 1979, and in southern Lebanon where a Shi'i militia has waged a lengthy guerrilla war against Israel and rival militias within Lebanon. In actual fact, much of Shi'i history has been one of political withdrawal and an outright rejection of worldly power. After the assassination of Ali in 661 and the martyrdom of his son Husayn in 680, the Shi'is were not to wield political power for quite some time, as a result of which they spent less time emphasizing the political dimension of Shi'ism and more on developing elaborate theological ideas. However, the early political experiences had a direct bearing on Shi'i beliefs, which emphasize the importance of martyrdom and persecution.

Sectarian Division

There are three main branches of Shi'ism, the **Twelver Shi'is**, **Isma'ilis**, and **Zaydis**, all of which are united by a common belief that the only legitimate leader of the Muslim community is a descendant of Ali and his wife **Fatima**, the daughter of the Prophet. This leader is known as the **Imam**, and is considered superior to other human beings on account of his bloodline. The three main Shi'i sects agree on the identities of the first four Imams. There is disagreement over the fifth, with the majority believing that Husayn's grandson, Muhammad al-Baqir (d. 731), was the rightful Imam, and a minority following al-Baqir's brother, Zayd (d. 740), on account of which they are called Zaydis.

Zaydis

Zayd was the first person after the massacre of Husayn and his family to try to wrest political power from the Umayyads by force. After spending a year in preparation in the heavily Shiʿi city of Kufa in Iraq, he came out with a group of followers but was killed in battle.

Zaydi beliefs are similar to those of the major Shiʿi sect, that of the Twelvers. The major difference is that Zaydis believe that any descendant of Ali and Fatima can be the Imam regardless of whether they are descended from Husayn or his elder brother Hasan. In order to be acknowledged as the Imam, a person must have the ability to resort to the sword if necessary. For this reason, unlike in Twelver Shiʿism, no person who remains hidden can be considered the rightful Imam. The Zaydi Imam is also required to possess high moral character and religious learning. If a person does not live up to all these requirements, he cannot be recognized as a full Imam but is an inferior Imam of either martial skill or learning only. Leaders whose political and intellectual strength is only enough to keep the Zaydi religious claim alive are called *Daʿis*, a term shared by the third Shiʿi sect, the Ismaʿilis. The high standards required of a Zaydi Imam, combined with the concept of the *Daʿi*, allows for the possibility that there might be an age without an Imam, when the community is led by *Daʿis*.

Zaydi Shiʿism never gained a great following and in modern times is almost entirely limited to Yemen.

Twelvers

Those members of the Shiʿi community who did not accept Zayd as the rightful Imam remained in agreement for two more generations. The sixth Imam of this group, **Jaʿfar al-Sadiq** (d. 765), is especially important because he was a very great scholar who is also highly regarded by the Sunnis. The major Shiʿi school of religious law is called "Jaʿfari" because of him.

After the death of Jaʿfar al-Sadiq this Shiʿi group divided into two, the first being Ismaʿilis, who recognized his elder son Ismaʿil (d. 765) as the rightful leader; the second followed his younger son, Musa (d. 799). This latter sect continued following a chain of Imams until the twelfth in succession from Ali, Muhammad al-Mahdi, vanished in 874 C.E. His followers, thereafter known as Twelver Shiʿis, believed that he had gone into a form of supernatural hiding and would return as the messiah at the end of the world.

Twelver Shiʿis have a complex theory concerning the nature of the Imam, which derives in large part from writings attributed to Jaʿfar al-Sadiq. In every age there is an Imam who represents God on earth, and who designates his successor by giving him a body of knowledge covering the inner and outer meanings of the Qur'an. The institution of the Imam is a covenant between God and human beings, and all believing Twelver Shi'is are required to acknowledge and follow the Imam of their age. Twelver Shi'is regard Imams as free of sin; they serve as the doorway to God and convey His message directly.

After the disappearance of the twelfth Imam, envoys (*wakils*) acting on his behalf claimed that they were in direct contact with him. When the fourth of them died in 939 C.E., no one else succeeded in his claim to be the *wakil* of the vanished Imam. The period from then on came to be known as the "Greater Occultation," as distinct from the earlier one, which was called the "Lesser Occultation." During this later period, which extends until today, Twelver Shi'ism developed an elaborate clerical system that takes care of the religious needs of the Shi'i community. The highest rank of this clergy is believed to be inspired by the Imam and is given the right to engage in independent reasoning, or *ijtihad*. In actual fact, since the sixteenth century, Shi'i clerics have been extremely conservative in their exercise of *ijtihad* and, for all practical purposes, act exactly the way a Sunni scholar does in the study of law.

Isma'ilis

Some Shi'is maintained that it was Isma'il and not his younger brother Musa who was the rightful seventh Imam, despite the fact that Isma'il died before his father, Ja'far al-Sadiq. According to Isma'ili doctrine, before dying Isma'il designated his son Muhammad ibn Isma'il as his successor, and the line of Imams continued with him.

A fundamental feature of early Isma'ili thought was the division of all knowledge into two levels, an outer, exoteric one (*zahir*) and an inner, esoteric one (*batin*). The exoteric level of knowledge changes with every prophet and every scripture. The esoteric level is concealed under the words of the scriptures and their laws, and conveys an immutable truth which can only be made apparent through a process of interpretation (called *ta'wil*). This is the exclusive prerogative of the Imam or else of his deputies.

One of the most interesting aspects of Isma'ili thought is the concept of cyclical time. History goes through a cycle of seven eras, each inaugurated by a prophet who publicly announces his message using a scripture. The first six of these prophets are Adam, Noah, Abraham, Moses, Jesus, and Muhammad. These prophets are accompanied by a silent companion who is the guardian of the esoteric dimension of the scripture. In the cycle of Muhammad, Muhammad ibn Isma'il is the sev-

This mud-brick mosque in Jenne, Mali, was constructed in the fourteenth century and is the oldest in Africa. The mud, which washes away in the rain, needs continual renewal—hence the built-in "scaffolding" of the structure.

enth Imam and will return in the future to serve as the public prophet of his own (the seventh) prophetic cycle, bringing the entire cycle of seven to an end and our world with it. Until his return, Isma'ilis believe that the hidden *batin* knowledge should be kept secret, and revealed only to initiated believers.

The Isma'ilis became extremely powerful in North Africa in the tenth century and founded a dynasty known as the Fatimids, which for a brief period posed a threat to the absolute political authority of the Sunni Caliphs of the **Abbasid** dynasty. The great city of Cairo was founded by these Isma'ilis, as was Cairo's famous university, **Al-Azhar**. In later times this university became one of the most important centers of Sunni learning and continues in that role to this day.

Over the centuries Isma'ilism has split into a number of different sects, especially the rival followers of the two brothers, Nizar (d. 1095) and al-Musta'li (d. 1101). The Fatimid rulers supported the religious claims of al-Musta'li, forcing the followers of Nizar to flee Fatimid territories or else to hide for fear of persecution.

The Fatimid Empire was destroyed by the rise to power of the Sunni Ayyubids, but not before Isma'ili scholars patronized by the Fatimids had left a lasting impact on Islamic philosophy and mysticism. Nizar's followers found refuge in the Syrian and Iranian mountains, and dispersed after the Mongol invasion of the thirteenth century. In the nineteenth century the Iranian monarch gave the well-known title Agha Khan to the Imam of one of their sub-sects, the Qasimshahis. Today Isma'ilis remain fragmented, with Nizaris concentrated in northern Pakistan as well as parts of Afghanistan, Tajikistan, and India. The line of al-Musta'li is concentrated around the Arabian Sea, on the western coast of India and in Pakistan and Yemen. Currently the Institute of Isma'ili Studies in Britain is pioneering the collation of Isma'ili literature and, together with others, is helping to reconcile the disparate Isma'ili sub-sects.

Theology, Law, and Mysticism | 3

From the time of the Umayyad Caliphs onward (661–750) virtually all Muslim areas, with the exception of Iran after the sixteenth century, have had a Sunni majority. Most of the areas that converted to Islam after its initial rapid expansion in the seventh and eighth centuries also adopted the Sunni version of the religion, as a result of which Sunni theology and law are widely regarded as representing the "orthodox" Islamic tradition.

The Umayyads proved to be great state builders as were the Abbasid Caliphs (750–1258) after them. The Abbasids, who on occasion tried to reconcile the Sunni–Shiʿi schism, were also active champions of scholarship and the arts. Their dynasty heralded a period of unprecedented prosperity in the Islamic world, the mythic glory of which has been immortalized in works such as *The One Thousand and One Nights* (more commonly known in English as *The Arabian Nights*). Their rule is also frequently referred to as the Classical Islamic Age, when the major points of religious doctrine, law, theology, and philosophy were addressed in ways that framed their discussion until modern times and, arguably, continue to shape the ideas and behavior of traditionalists.

In this chapter I attempt to furnish a brief overview of some of the key developments in Islamic theology, law, and mysticism. It is impossible to provide a comprehensive account of these large subjects in such a brief space, but their central aspects, particularly those formulated in the Classical period, are easily outlined. One must bear in mind that the intricate details of theological and legal debates have little direct bearing on the religious lives of most Muslims. Nonetheless, over a period of time theological ideas have some influence in society, just as societal practices affect the content and nature of scholarly debate. More importantly, members of society can be directly affected by developments in law inasmuch as they see Islamic law as a guiding principle in their lives and are subjected to it by the judicial and police powers of a state.

Theology

As a prophet, Muhammad's role was more that of a preacher than a theologian. However, the Qur'an brings up many philosophical and theological questions regarding the nature of God, God's relationship to our world, the problem of evil, and the place occupied by human beings in the divine plan for the universe. As the Islamic world expanded to absorb new cultures many new philosophical questions emerged. Some of these issues were already being discussed in the newly converted territories; others were brought up by the theological debates that occurred as Islam came into competition with Christianity and Zoroastrianism, which were the major religions of that region; still others emerged as a result of political and social crises that plagued the early Muslim community.

The term most commonly used for theology in the Islamic world is *Kalam*, which literally means "speech" or "dialectic." This gives a clear sense of the fact that Islamic theology emerged in an environment where theological issues were being publicly debated. *Kalam* is distinct from Islamic philosophy, in that the philosophical tradition derived very consciously and directly from the world of Greek (and, to a lesser extent, Persian) thought. This is evident even from the word used for philosophy, which is *Falsafa*, an Arabic adaptation of the Greek word *philosophia*.

Many of the major questions that were discussed in the earliest Islamic theological circles arose out of the political crises that followed the assassinations of the Caliphs Umar, Uthman, and Ali, and from the civil wars that resulted in the division between the Sunni and Shi'i sects. The main questions dealt with who was the rightful leader of the community, and what was the status of a believer who committed a grave sin (since the killers of the early Caliphs were all Muslims). As theological schools grew within the Islamic world, the questions being debated became more theoretical and abstract. The main issues concerned the relationship between God's omnipotence and human responsibility. This led to more abstract discussions of the nature of God and of how human beings gained the ability to differentiate between right and wrong and to commit good and bad actions.

After the murder of Uthman and the emergence of sectarian divisions in the Islamic world, four major schools of thought emerged, representing the spectrum of Islamic theological opinions. The first of these, the **Qadariya**, were the most actively opposed to the Umayyad dynasty. The Qadariya believed that human beings have such extensive power over their actions that they can determine the commission and outcome of their acts. It is from the belief in human ability or determination (*qudra*) that the Qadariya get their name. Since human beings had complete freedom of action, and their deeds were a perfect mirror of their belief, anyone who committed a grave sin must be a disbeliever.

The second group were called the **Jabriya**, who took a diametrically opposite view to the original Qadariya. They believed that divine compulsion (*jabr*) created human actions and that human beings had absolutely no freedom in committing good or bad actions. Since God was the direct source of all acts, a human being could not be held responsible for committing a grave sin and therefore would still be considered a Muslim.

The Murji'a occupied a position in-between the Qadariya and the Jabriya. They believed that it was not possible for human beings to pass judgment over the status of another human being's faith. Instead, based on a Qur'anic verse, they believed that a grave sinner's future was held in suspense awaiting God's decision.

The last major group was called the Khawarij. Like the Qadariya, they believed that actions were the perfect mirror of an individual's faith; unlike them, however, they tended to be extremely politically active. They felt it was the duty of every true Muslim to depose, by force if necessary, any leader who had strayed from the correct path. They also believed that any Muslim male, regardless of whether he belonged to Muhammad's tribe or not, could be declared Caliph as long as he was of irreproachable moral character. The Khawarij had originally supported Ali in his competition with Mu'awiya, but when Ali agreed to human arbitration (as opposed to letting God make the decision on the battlefield), they deserted him and came to be very distinct from his supporters, the Shi'is.

By the end of the eighth century these early trends had developed to the point that full-fledged theological schools had emerged within the Islamic world. The most famous of these is called the **Mu'tazila**, which for forty years in the mid ninth century held sway as the official theological school of the Sunni world. Many religious scholars were mistreated if their beliefs did not tally with those of the Mu'tazila. But when the Mu'tazila lost their official patronage, they came to be seen as heretical and were themselves victims of discrimination and persecution. This period of "inquisition" did nonetheless produce one benefit—a greater formalization of Islamic thought. The Muʿtazila were largely replaced by the **Ashʿariya** school, named for a scholar called **al-Ashʿari** (d. 935), a disillusioned former Muʿtazila theologian.

The two schools took quite different stands on a range of issues. For instance, whereas the Muʿtazila saw God's attributes (for example references in the Qurʾan to His compassion and mercy, even His hands and throne) as distinct from His essence and therefore non-eternal, the Ashʿariya believed that God does indeed have eternal attributes, such as knowledge, sight, and speech. To the Ashʿariya, such anthropomorphic qualities are real—it is just that we humans cannot understand their true meaning. Similarly, the Ashʿariya regard the Qurʾan as the eternal speech of God, while the Muʿtazila believe that it might be replaced at some future date, if God so willed.

Unlike the Muʿtazila, the Ashʿariya implicitly accepted the vision of God that is promised in the afterlife. They also believed that the omnipotent God had willed both good and evil in the world. At the same time, the Ashʿariya felt that humans were accountable for their actions. From this they deduced that sinners could remain Muslim, yet still be punished in Hell for their crimes.

These differences between the Muʿtazila and Ashʿariya hinged on their different understandings of the power of human reason. The Ashʿariya recognize that human beings have some degree of free will and power of reasoning, but feel that these human abilities are extremely limited when compared to the omniscience and omnipotence of God. The Muʿtazila, on the other hand, had great faith in the powers of the human intellect and refused to accept that certain things lay beyond human understanding. Both these positions have bases in the Islamic philosophical tradition, from which Islamic theology derived many of its ideas.

Islamic Law: Shariʿa

Islamic religious law is an elaborate and dynamic system that has been evolving from the time of Muhammad until the present. It continues to be taken very seriously by a large number of Muslims, who use its rules and values as guiding principles in their lives. They consider the law to be one of the most remarkable aspects of their religion.

Sources

Islamic law (*Shari'a*) is believed to be the collected prescriptions dictated by God for the running of the universe. The Qur'an provides very clear rules on issues as diverse as how to perform acts of worship, what not to eat, and how to distribute inheritance property. However, it does not provide clear rules for all of the innumerable situations encountered in the course of human life. The Islamic community did not see this as a problem when they had the living example of the Prophet to follow. Nor did the generations immediately after the death of Muhammad, because his memory was very much alive in the community: people felt they had a good idea of what Muhammad would have done in any given situation. However, as generations passed and the Islamic community spread to new cultures and was faced with new situations, it was more and more difficult to use the practices of Muhammad to guide all aspects of life. It therefore became necessary to develop a system of law that provided a method by which rules could be developed to deal with new situations. This system is called *Fiqh* and is considered to have four principles called *Usul al-fiqh* (Principles of Jurisprudence), namely the Qur'an, *Sunna*, reasoning by analogy (*qiyas*), and consensus of the community (*ijma*).

Principles of Jurisprudence

The primary source of Islamic law is the Qur'an. Rules and precepts that are clearly stated in the Qur'an are not open to debate and must be accepted at face value. Thus, for example, since the Qur'an explicitly forbids the eating of pork, *Shari'a*-observing Muslims see no need to consult other authorities.

If the Qur'an does not provide clear rules on a question of law, then one looks to the example of the Prophet or his *Sunna*. Often translated as "tradition," *Sunna* is the way Muhammad lived his life (see p. 24). This is preserved as "living *Sunna*" in the traditions of a virtuous Islamic community and as "recorded *Sunna*" in the anecdotes concerning Muhammad's actions, which are known as hadiths. The concept of *Sunna* is open to interpretation, since the vast number of individual hadiths sometimes contradict one another; furthermore, the concept of "living tradition" can cause conflict because not everyone agrees on which traditions of a society are in keeping with what Muhammad would have done and which are innovations. From the ninth century onward Muslim jurists have struggled to balance the Qur'an and *Sunna*, and to derive laws from these sources that can then be applied to new situations. This normally involves reasoning by analogy (the third Principle of

Jurisprudence) and consensus of the community (the fourth). This system of independent legal reasoning to come up with new laws is called *ijtihad*, and someone who is qualified to engage in it is called a *mujtahid*.

Sunni Muslim jurists belong to four schools that differ as to whether or not they put more trust in the textual sources of Qur'an and Hadith, or in the human ability to reason by analogy. These schools are called the Maliki, Hanbali, Hanafi, and Shafi'i. The **Maliki** school is traditionally strongest in North Africa and considers the "living *Sunna*" of the community to be more reliable than human reason. The **Hanbali** school is strongest in Saudi Arabia; it has historically given a great deal of weight to the literal interpretation of written texts, so much so that some Hanbali scholars insisted that an unreliable hadith should be preferred over a strong example of reasoning by analogy.

The **Shafi'i** and **Hanafi** schools together account for the majority of Sunni Muslims and have a wide distribution, the Shafi'i school being more popular among the Arabs of the Middle East and in Indonesia, and the Hanafi school being more accepted in South and Central Asia and in Turkey. Since the sixteenth century, the Hanafi school has largely replaced the Shafi'i school as the most influential legal tradition in the Islamic world. The Hanafi and Shafi'i schools use the principle of *ijtihad* to a much greater degree than do the Hanbali and Maliki schools.

The best way to explain how the Principles of Jurisprudence work is to use an example, such as whether or not it is permissible to use a loudspeaker to make the Islamic call to prayer. Of course, neither the Qur'an nor the Hadith has any explicit reference to loudspeakers (or any other electrical device). On the other hand, there are several places in the Qu'ran where one is encouraged to pray. There are also hadith accounts that state that the Prophet appointed a particular person named Bilal to make the call to prayer because of his strong and attractive voice, and that this man used to stand on high ground to make the call so that it would carry further. Reasoning by analogy, a legal scholar would argue that the Qur'an encourages prayer as an activity, and that the Prophet appointed Bilal to make the call to prayer precisely so that his voice would reach out to the widest possible audience. That Bilal stood on high ground also indicates that the Prophet wanted the call to prayer to reach as far as possible. Since a loudspeaker in no way changes the call to prayer but only makes it louder, thereby allowing it to be heard by more people, it should be permitted by Islamic law. If there was little or no objection to this legal opinion and several other judges arrived at a similar decision, there would be a consensus of opinion over the use of loudspeakers in making the call to prayer and they would be accepted by Islamic law (as, in fact, they have been).

In practice, by the fourteenth century, many parts of the Islamic world had developed specialized offices dealing with the practice of law. The scholar who engaged in the theoretical study and interpretation of Islamic law was called a *faqih*. People with questions concerning the law would go to someone called a **mufti**, who was normally appointed by the ruler for the specific purpose of answering questions concerning the *Shari'a*. At other times, the *mufti* was a highly-respected *faqih* who became a *mufti* simply because he gained a reputation among the local populace as a good, reliable scholar. The *mufti*'s answer to questions is called a **fatwa**, best translated as a legal opinion or decree. In theory, the *mufti*'s opinion is binding on the person who posed the legal question. In practice, people frequently ignore the *mufti*'s opinion if it displeases them, largely because there is no institution that enforces his decision. The office of a judge, that is, someone who presides over a court and has the power of the state and its police to enforce his opinions, is fulfilled by a **qadi**. Qadis are government officials and are appointed by the rulers. Many *faqihs* consider government employment to be inappropriate for a scholar of law, because of the temptation to compromise in matters of principle.

The system of Islamic law, or *Shari'a*, attempts to regulate all aspects of human life. It divides activities into the ritual and devotional acts by which human beings communicate with God (called *ibadat*, meaning acts of worship or servanthood) and the myriad details of relationships between human beings (called *mu'amalat*). In an attempt to take a comprehensive position on all aspects of human life, legal scholars have created a scale upon which they judge every human activity, be it ritual or interpersonal. At one extreme lie those activities—most of which are ritual obligations—which all *Shari'a*-observing Muslims are required to do; at the other end of the scale are behaviors that are categorically forbidden, such as worshiping a deity other than Allah. Key points on the scale between these two extremes are occupied by actions that are recommended (for example showing hospitality to strangers) and those that are discouraged (for example being cruel to animals).

There is considerable regional variation in what is understood to be permissible and forbidden under *Shari'a* law, particularly in dietary matters. On occasion, these differences derive from the distinctive legal traditions of various schools, although the schools' attitudes toward the permissibility of edible items is often determined by the region's food habits or dietary history. Furthermore, it is doubtful whether the average Muslim resident of a particular locale makes the distinction between what is normative within his or her own region's legal tradition and what is normative for Islam as a whole. Thus many Sunni Muslims from the west coast of India consider lobster, crabs, and mollusks forbidden (a belief shared by Twelver Shi'is); but Muslims from Turkey and Lebanon, while sharing the Hanafi legal school with the Indians, consider all food from the sea to be permissible.

Although many Muslims are not consciously aware of the degree to which Islamic beliefs and practices vary from one cultural context to another, the *Shari'a* legal tradition is based upon liberal accommodation to the particularities of context. Scholars of the stature of al-Shafi'i (d. 820, after whom the Shafi'i school is named) and al-Shaybani (d. 805, possibly the most influential figure in the Hanafi school) insisted that jurists should never rely completely on legal precedent but should look at the details of each case that comes before them, because the circumstances of every individual are unique. This attitude toward law has prevented *Shari'a* from developing as a codified legal system. Some modern Islamic countries have attempted to formalize the *Shari'a* in order to use it as a national legal code on the model of European ones, but they have met with limited success.

The focus on the individual in Islamic law gives it a mediatory character as opposed to the inquisitorial one of Western law. Unlike the Western system, in which individuals are normally accused by a corporate entity, such as a state or society, whose interests transcend those of the individual, Islamic legal processes traditionally mediate between individuals in which either one party or both parties might accuse the other of a legal transgression. This function of the judge demands certain interpersonal skills and also means that the desired goal of the process is arriving at a settlement, not reaching a verdict. The personal and contextual nature of Islamic law sounds as if it would be more fair than a codified legal system. But critics say that, in practice, the realities of overburdened legal systems and less than conscientious judges mean that people who are unfamiliar with the law have fewer safeguards than if they were subject to a rigid legal code.

There is a historical bias in favor of seeing the legal aspects of Islam as the core of the tradition. As a result Islam is sometimes caricatured as a dry, ritualistic religion that emphasizes legal conformity in one's public behavior over what one believes or does in private. This skewed perspective probably stems from the fact that the ritual and legal aspects of Islam are naturally more visible than personal beliefs, and also from the greater exposure and influence the practice of *Shari'a* derives from its close relationship with the instruments of state. In practice, even the most ardent champions of Islamic jurisprudence have seen it as only one facet of their religion. Other scholars have explicitly stated that blind devotion to scholastic traditions of law and philosophy do not represent the core of a fulfilled religious life, and that faith and piety are more important. The most famous advocate of this viewpoint is al-Ghazali (d. 1111), who spent most of his adult life as a professor of theology. In 1095, while at the height of his professorial career, he suffered a severe emotional crisis that caused him to leave his job in Baghdad and return to his home town, where he devoted himself to a life of contemplation. He eventually came to the conclusion that rational and philosophical inquiry can carry a person only so far, and that achieving complete understanding requires a leap of faith. This leap of faith was best achieved through mystical training and experience, something commonly referred to as **Sufism**.

Mystical Islam: Sufism

Sufism is an umbrella term for a variety of philosophical, social, and literary phenomena occurring within the Islamic world. In its narrowest sense, the term refers to a number of schools of Islamic mystical philosophy and theology, to religious orders and guilds that have greatly influenced the development of Islamic politics and society, and to the varied expressions of popular piety and shrine-cults found throughout the Islamic world. In a wider sense, Sufism is often seen as the spiritual muse behind much of pre-modern verse in the Islamic world, the idiom of much of popular Islamic piety, the primary social arena open to women's religious participation, and a major force in the conversion of people to Islam in Africa and Asia. Sufi orders served as educational institutions that fostered not only the religious sciences but also music and decorative arts. Sometimes Sufi leaders served as theologians and judges, combining within themselves scholastic and charismatic forms of leadership; at other times, they led the challenge against the legal and theological establishment. In modern times (as at other periods in history), the Sufi orders have been praised for their capacity to serve as channels for religious reform. At the same time, they have been criticized for a lack of respect for Islamic law, and for fostering ignorance and superstition in order to maintain their control over the community.

The origins of Sufism lie in a very informal movement of personal piety that emerged in the first century of Islam. These earliest Sufis emphasized prayer, asceticism, and withdrawal from society. The term "Sufism"—or *tasawwuf* as the tradition is called in Arabic—may derive from the practice of wearing wool (*suf* in Arabic), or possibly from the Arabic word for purity (*safa*). The earliest Sufis spent almost all their waking hours in prayer, and frequently engaged in acts of self-mortification, such as starving themselves or staying up the entire night, as a form of prayer exercise. They renounced their connections to the world and possessed little apart from the clothes on their backs. A large proportion of these early Sufis were women, several of whom, such as Rabi'a al-Adawiya (d. 801), are revered to this day.

It is very likely that the Sufis adopted the practices of asceticism and the wearing of wool after observing the Christian ascetics of Syria and Palestine. Sufis, however, see the origins of their movement in the Qur'an and in the life of Muhammad. They are quick to observe that Muhammad lived an extremely simple, almost ascetic, life, and that he had a habit of withdrawing from Mecca to go and meditate in a cave. Indeed, it was while he was meditating in this manner that he received his first revelation. Sufis therefore see their practices as an imitation of Muhammad, and they hope to achieve the same close relationship with God as he did.

According to Islamic belief, all Muslims will have a direct encounter with God after they die (opinions differ as to what this means), but Sufis do not wish to wait that long. This desire is expressed in a saying attributed to the Prophet and very popular in Sufi circles that encourages Muslims to "Die before you die."

The direct experience of God is considered so overwhelming as to be inexpressible and can be spoken about only in metaphors. The most commonly used metaphors are those of falling in love and of being intoxicated with wine. These images are frequently encountered in Sufi literature, particularly in poetry which tries to express the indescribable joy that Sufis experience through their relationship with God, combined with the heartache of being separated from Him. The following work by the Ottoman poetess Mihri Hatun (d. c. 1512) is but one example of a vast, rich literature that spans all the languages spoken by Muslims:

At times, my longing for the beloved slays me
At times, union with him and the passing of time slay me too
My enemy laughs at my condition, but I cry on and on

How can my spirit endure this sorrow which kills us all?
Oh you who doctors the sick heart with his image
The trouble is medicines, like poison, kill me
This day, all my friends and enemies, come crying
I've not yet met my fated end, but these perplexities kill me
Oh my rival, if Mihri dies on the thorn of love, why grieve?
You dog! The grave-keeper stones you, but the rose-mouthed one
    slays him too[1]

The Sufi concept of union with God is expressed in many different ways. The main problem in Sufi philosophical circles is: How can a mortal human being unite with the omnipotent, omniscient deity who is unlike us in every way? The union with God is normally called *fana*, which literally means destruction or annihilation. Sufis believe that in the final stage of an individual's spiritual development, she loses any consciousness of her individual identity, and is only aware of the identity of God. In effect, God's identity then replaces the identity of the Sufi.

There is disagreement among Sufis over whether the final spiritual goal of Sufism is to lose one's identity completely in the identity of God, or to reach a stage where one's own petty concerns no longer prevent us from seeing the world in its true nature. A common metaphor for the first approach is to describe the Sufi's individuality as a drop which vanishes into the ocean; it does not actually cease to exist, for it is now part of the vastness of the sea; it only ceases to exist insofar as it is an individual drop. The latter view, that one sees things more clearly, depicts the human heart (considered the seat of the intellect in medieval Islamic thought) as a mirror that is normally dirty, tarnished by our everyday concerns and petty desires. Through engaging in mystical exercises we effectively polish the mirrors of our hearts and cleanse them to the point where they can accurately reflect the light of God.

The Sufi Path

Sufis believe that average human beings are unable to understand the true nature of spirituality because of their petty concerns. The quest for spiritual understanding in Sufism is seen as a path, which each Sufi must travel under the guidance of a teacher or master. This path has many stages, the number and names of which vary depending on the school of Sufi thought. In most instances, the first stage on the Sufi path is one of repentance. The Sufi is expected to repent of all the bad deeds he or she has committed in life and to take a vow to avoid all earthly pleasures.

After having repented of the past, the Sufi is supposed to divest him- or herself of earthly belongings, which even include attachments to friends and family. After having done so, Sufis traditionally enter a monastery or convent and devote themselves fully to the difficult task of shedding earthly concerns. In practice, this process of divestment is extremely difficult, often takes a long time, and requires strict, meditational exercises under the directions of a master.

The Sufi path relies on meditation to accomplish its goals. The various Sufi forms of meditation are called *dhikr* (or *zikr*). *Dhikr* literally means "repetition," "remembrance," "utterance," or "mentioning"; in the Qur'an it appears in the context of urging Muslims to remember their Lord frequently. At its most basic level, Sufi *dhikr* consists of repeating one of God's names over and over. In Islam, God is believed to have many names that describe some aspect of his nature. Of these, ninety-nine are considered special and are called the "Most Beautiful Names." The name of God used most frequently in *dhikr* exercises is "Allah" (which Sufis see as the most excellent name), although others, such as *Rahim* (Merciful) or *Wahid* (Unique) are also used. The purpose of reciting these names is to concentrate wholly on what one is doing and to lose all self-awareness. One's entire being becomes permeated with the *dhikr* formula through repetition, so that even if one ceases actively to engage in *dhikr*, it continues to be repeated in one's heart.

Some *dhikr* exercises involve the repetition of longer formulas, while others also entail complicated methods of breath control. An example of a relatively simple *dhikr* exercise involving breath control requires the Sufi to say out loud a bisyllabic name of God (such as "*Wahid*," meaning "The Unique"), inhaling on the first syllable and exhaling on the second. This practice is called the "Sawing *dhikr*," because the distinctive sound made by speaking while inhaling and then while exhaling resembles the noise made by a saw as it cuts through wood. Other forms of *dhikr* are much more complicated, such as one that involves reciting the formula "There is no god but God" in a long breath broken up into five beats. Such complex meditational exercises were very difficult to learn on one's own, and only became popular after the master–disciple relationship had evolved to the point that Sufis were organized into hierarchical Sufi orders, called *tariqas*.

Organized Sufism: The Sufi Orders

By the thirteenth century, Islamic educational and legal institutions had been formalized, as had the relationship between the government and theological and legal scholars. It is therefore no surprise that Sufism would also take an organized form and compete for social legitimacy and authority with other religious movements and institutions.

The earliest Sufi orders were made up of the disciples of a particular master; after these disciples had themselves become accomplished Sufis, they imparted their master's teachings to their own students. So began the tradition of students following in the lineage of an initial master, and emulating his *tariqa* (path), an organizational system which became formalized by the fifteenth century. Before an aspirant Sufi could join an order, he would often be turned away repeatedly to test his sincerity, or forced to perform menial tasks as a process of initiation. Admission into an order was normally a ceremonial occasion, when new members would be given robes signifying their new status.

Many Sufi orders have been extremely important in the evolution of Islamic society. Not only did they have prominent scholars and philosophers developing their ideas, but frequently major figures in the government belonged to these orders. This meant that Sufi orders could influence the official policies of the kingdom. Three such orders deserve special attention: the Chishti, Mevlevi, and Naqshbandi.

The **Chishti** order takes its named from Khaja Mu'in al-Din Chishti (d. 1235), who came from a town in Afghanistan and settled in the city of Ajmer in India, where he taught a large number of influential disciples. These disciples of Khaja Chishti opened Chishti centers in provincial towns all over India; they also had many rulers, princes, and princesses as their disciples, and rapidly became the most influential order in India. The Chishti order has as its *dhikr* a particular kind of musical performance called *qawwali*, in which a group of musicians sing religious songs set to a very rhythmic beat. The late Pakistani singer, Nusrat Fateh Ali Khan (d. 1997), whose fame spread to the West, was the best-known modern exponent of the *qawwali*.

The **Mevlevi** order is largely limited to the Turkish and Balkan areas of the Ottoman Empire (thirteenth to early twentieth century). Its members became well known in Europe as the "Whirling Dervishes," on account of their distinctive *dhikr* ritual. The order derives its name from the famous mystical poet Jalal al-Din Rumi (d. 1273), called Mevlana in Turkish. Rumi was born in Central Asia and moved to Turkey in 1219, where his father was appointed a professor of legal thought in Konya, the seat of the Seljuk rulers. Rumi inherited this post after his father's death. In 1244 he fell under the spell of a wandering mystic named Shams-e Tabrizi, and after the latter's mysterious disappearance, Rumi

Sufism represents a mystical, contemplative strand of Islam—a strand captured vividly by the Mevlevi order (known by Westerners as "whirling dervishes"). Their slow, revolving dance is a ritual that helps to create higher states of consciousness.

devoted himself to the guidance of Sufi disciples and the writing of poetry.

A distinctive feature of the Mevlevi order is the importance given to music and dance in their *dhikr* practices. The Mevlevi meditational exercise, called **sema**, involves the recitation of prayers and hymns, after which the participants make several rounds of the hall, in a dance with their arms extended sideways, the right palm facing upwards and the left downwards, and whirl counterclockwise, using their left feet as a pivot. The *sema* symbolizes the simultaneous receipt of divine grace and its transmission to humanity. The Mevlevi order has emphasized art and culture since Rumi's day, and has inspired both court poets in Ottoman times and young musicians and poets in modern Turkey.

Unlike the Mevlevi and Chishti orders, which are both geographically and ethnically limited in range, the **Naqshbandi** order is distributed widely throughout the Islamic world. It is named after a Central Asian Sufi scholar from the city of Bukhara in Uzbekistan named Baha al-Din Naqshband (d. 1389). Naqshbandis believe that Sufis should not withdraw from society but should pursue their spiritual goals while fulfilling all their social responsibilities. They hold eight principles to be central to their order: awareness while breathing, watching one's steps, journeying within, solitude within human society, recollection, restraining one's thoughts, watching one's thoughts, and concentration on the Divine.

Naqshbandi figures were very important in religious reform movements in the eighteenth and nineteenth centuries, particularly in India and Central Asia where Muslims were fighting British and Russian colonialism, respectively. In the twentieth century, a whole host of Naqshbandi groups encouraged the Turkish-speaking subject peoples of the Soviet Union to resist Russian domination. Today, many Naqshbandis provide education and social services in the Central Asian and Caucasian countries that emerged after the Soviet Union's collapse. In recent years one branch of the Naqshbandis, that of Shaykh Nazim and his designated successor, Shaykh Hisham Kabbani, has become active in Muslim circles in the United States. Their supporters welcome their apolitical stress on piety and ecumenism; their critics see them as undermining the Islamic emphasis on individual empowerment by concentrating on the cult of personality surrounding the Sufi master.

Veneration of Saints

One of the most frequent criticisms levelled against Sufism is that most Sufi practice elevates individual shaykhs or *pirs* (as Sufi figures are often called in non-Arab societies) to a superhuman level, accords them miraculous powers, and encourages ordinary people to devote themselves entirely to these masters. Despite the fact that many strict interpretations of Islam reject the notion that any class of human beings has the power to intercede with God on behalf of ordinary Muslims, the overwhelming majority of Muslims believe in and venerate saints in a variety of ways. There are two main types of saints, the first of which is made up of members of Muhammad's family, whose shrines are visited by both Shi'is and Sunnis, who hold the family of Muhammad in high regard. The second type consists of important Sufi figures whose shrines become famous at a local or regional level as a place where prayers have a good chance of being answered. An example of a local saint would be Telli Baba (literally, "Father Tinsel"), whose shrine situated just to the north of Istanbul, Turkey, is visited by women looking for a husband. The strange name of the shrine derives from the pieces of tinsel that cover the tomb. Visitors take a piece of tinsel from the shrine, and when their wishes are granted they return with an offering of money and a handful of tinsel to add to the tomb.

Innumerable local shrines of this type can be found across the Islamic world. Other Sufi shrines have an international importance and are visited by millions of people, particularly on festivals which commemorate the birth or death of the saint. These include the shrine of Mu'in al-Din Chishti in Ajmer, India, and Sayyida Zaynab (the great, great, great grand-daughter of the Prophet) in Cairo.

The key ingredient in the charisma of a saint is the possession of a quality called *baraka*, a miraculous power that is bestowed on human beings by God. *Baraka* gives its possessors curative and mediatory powers, enabling them not only to intercede before God on behalf of their devotees but also to solve social, economic, physical, and spiritual problems. It functions as an almost physical commodity and is contagious inasmuch as it is normally passed from a saint to his or her descendants or to a designated successor. For the most part, however, *baraka* is transmitted only within families, and a saint's successor who is not a blood relative is normally understood to have possessed "latent" *baraka* that was brought to the fore by association with the saint. Followers or devotees of a saint make supplications and offerings in order to acquire some of his *baraka*, although the kind they possess is not contagious; in other words, *baraka* rubs off from a saint onto individual followers, but this *baraka* never gets translated into their own and cannot be transferred to others.

Mysticism and Magic

Magic is an awkward concept for many Muslims, for it implies that supernatural powers do not ultimately derive from God—a clearly heretical stance. Nonetheless, magic does undeniably permeate the lives of many Muslims for whom a world without *jinn* (demonic beings) and magical powers is inconceivable. For instance, within clear sight of an affluent section of the Moroccan capital of Rabat stand the ruins of the Phoenician city of Sala, where, sandwiched between an egret rookery and a clump of banana trees, lies a square pond of pre-Islamic design. The pond contains a colony of eels that are fed eggs by visiting women as an aid to conceiving a child. Next to the pond are a number of Islamic tombs from the fourteenth-century Merenid period, the presence of which establishes a direct link between the offerings made at the pond and the curative powers of these shrines.

In the Mediterranean and west Asian worlds most magical practices engaged in by Muslims are to ward off the Evil Eye.[2] It is quite common for extremely well-educated Turks to practice regular rituals and carry blue talismans to ward off the Evil Eye, and in Pakistan in the 1990s investors have paraded rams through the Karachi Stock Exchange floor and then sacrificed them in order to reverse an inexplicable slide in the stock market. Belief in the Evil Eye is integrally linked with people's understanding of the Qur'an; the short, final three chapters are frequently recited for the express purpose of warding off the Evil Eye, and people commonly recite certain other verses of the Qur'an, wear talismans (called *ta°widh*) made out of them, or ritualistically consume or burn them. The preparation and acquisition of talismans is strongly associated with Sufi shrines and there is a direct correlation between the potency accorded to a talisman and the reputation as a miracle worker, or the *baraka*, of the person providing it.

Conclusion

At first glance, the legal, theological, and mystical traditions of Islam seem to be disparate and lacking in any overlapping functions and concerns. In actual fact, they evolved in constant interaction with one another, each influencing the other's development. Throughout Islamic history, prominent scholars of theology have also been renowned as respected mystics; likewise, masters of a Sufi order have functioned as the legal authorities in their communities. This lack of rigid delineation between religious specializations has allowed for the easier integration of the intellectual tradition into everyday life.

Muslims have a number of highly developed rituals and beliefs, all of which are seen as having their basis in the Qur'an and the life of Muhammad. They were further developed by legal scholars and theologians at different times and in different cultural contexts, which may explain why there is so much variation in observance of rituals, and even in Muslims' understanding of the fundamental texts of the faith.

Most of the rituals and doctrines outlined in this chapter are those of the Sunni sect, which accounts for the overwhelming majority of Muslims, although even the Sunnis have some differences. These are most striking in rituals concerning birth, marriage, and other festivals marking passage through life; however, they are also apparent in the practice of rituals, such as prayer.

Pillars of the Faith

Muslims are supposed to believe in five cardinal points, which are so central to the religion that they are called the "Pillars of Faith." These are Divine Unity, Prophecy, Revelation, Angelic Agency, and the existence of an Afterlife.

Divine Unity

Muslims believe in the oneness of God, a concept known by its Arabic name as *tawhid*. The term *tawhid* not only refers to the concept of God's unity but also to the affirmation of this unity by human beings. In other words, the notion of *tawhid* makes human beings active participants in ensuring that God remains understood as a unique being and thus crucial actors in God's relationship with the world.

The unique nature of God is frequently attested to in the Qur'an. Two short sections of the scripture are particularly valuable in providing

a general understanding of how God is viewed by the majority of
Muslims. The first of these constitutes a very brief chapter in its entirety and is called "Sincerity" (*Ikhlas, Chapter 112*):

> Say, He is God, the One and Only
> God, the Eternal, Absolute;
> He begets not, nor is He begotten;
> And there is none like unto Him.

The second is a single verse in a much longer chapter (2:255):

> God! There is no God but Him, the Living, the Eternal. No
> slumber can seize Him nor sleep. His are all things in the
> heavens and on earth. Who is there can intercede in His
> presence except as He permits? He knows what is before
> them and what after [or behind] them. Nor shall they
> compass aught of His knowledge except as He wills. His
> throne extends over the heavens and the earth, and He feels
> no fatigue in guarding and preserving them, for He is the
> Most High, the Supreme [in glory].

As is clearly emphasized by these selections from the Qur'an, God is
unique and eternal. He exists in and of Himself and has no needs. For
reasons that are inscrutable to human beings, God created the universe
and all that exists within it; He created human beings and gave them the
capacity to do good as well as evil, and the ability to choose between the
two. Human beings can know God through His attributes (such as
mercy, justice, compassion, wrath, and so on), but the ultimate essence
of God remains unknowable. According to Islamic understanding, God
has no body and is unlike anything in the created world. Furthermore, it
is a very grave sin to consider anything as an equal or companion of God.
There has been, nonetheless, a substantial debate among Muslim theologians and philosophers over whether or not God is similar enough to
human beings for us to be able to use anthropomorphic language to
describe Him.[1]

Prophecy

Muslims are supposed to believe that God wishes to communicate with
human beings, and that He uses prophets for this purpose. Prophets are
of two types, the first being those who have a mission from God to warn

their communities and acquaint them with God's will; these are referred to as *anbiya* (singular: *nabi*). The second category, in addition to fulfilling all the functions of the first group, is also given a revealed scripture that is supposed to be conveyed to their community. This special category of *anbiya* are called *rusul* (singular: *rasul*, meaning "messenger"). Muslims believe in a series of prophets which includes all the prophets mentioned in the Hebrew Bible as well as Jesus and Muhammad. The belief in Muhammad's role as the last prophet has emerged as a key tenet of Islamic dogma and is used as an important yardstick by which Islamic orthodoxy is judged. For instance, the major reason why many Sunnis consider the **Ahmadiya**, the followers of Mirza Ghulam Ahmad Qadian (d. 1908), apostates is that they grant him the status of prophethood. At times the emphasis seems to be primarily semantic, since Shi'i beliefs grant the Imam a religious role that often appears more important than that of any prophet; yet the Sunni majority regard them with less disfavor than they do the Ahmadiya, who are completely Sunni in matters of ritual and practice.[2]

Muslims consider Jesus to have been the second last prophet, who foretold the coming of Muhammad. The majority of Sunnis also consider Jesus to be the messiah and believe in the Virgin Birth. They do not, however, take this to mean that God was Jesus' father, but rather that God performed a miracle by causing Mary to conceive without a biological father.

Revelation

Muslims believe that God uses His prophets to reveal scriptures to humanity. Four such scriptures are recognized: the Torah as revealed to Moses, the Psalms of David, the New Testament of Jesus, and the Qur'an of Muhammad. According to Muslim belief, God's message is eternal and the substance of all these books is therefore the same. Differences between them are either explained by the fact that, after their revelation, earlier scriptures were tampered with by people who claimed to believe in them, or else by using a concept of human evolution. According to this theory, God always knew what He wished to teach humanity; however, humanity was not always ready for the full message. For this reason God revealed His message in progressively more comprehensive versions, culminating in the Qur'an, which is the definitive version of God's message, valid until the end of civilization.

Scripture is central to the Muslim understanding of religion; Jews and Christians are therefore referred to as "People of the Book" (*Ahl al-*

kitab), and their religions are recognized as divinely sanctioned, allowing Muslims to engage in social interaction with them.

Angelic Agency

Muslims are supposed to believe that angels exist and that they are used by God to perform His will. One of their duties is to watch over individual human beings and keep a record of all their actions. The most famous angel is Gabriel, who served as an intermediary between God and Muhammad in the revelation of the Qur'an. Another important figure is Iblis, who used to be the chief of all angels but was punished for disobeying God by being cast out of Heaven. After that he was turned into Satan and now not only rules Hell but also tries to tempt human beings from the path of goodness.

Many Muslims consider belief in angels to be the most difficult of the Pillars of Faith and explain them away as natural forces or different aspects of God's power. Others, however, have a complex belief in a variety of supernatural beings including angels and demons (normally but not exclusively called *jinn*), who interact with human beings in different ways, both malevolent and therapeutic.

Judgment and Afterlife

Muslims believe that our world will eventually come to an end and that we will be judged and rewarded or punished in the afterlife according to our actions on earth. Judgment, reward, and punishment are central points in Islam and are the foundation upon which its entire system of ethics is based. It is therefore no surprise that Islam has a highly developed system of eschatology (or theory of the end of the world), much of which is an elaboration of several very dramatic passages in the Qur'an.

> The Day of noise and clamor:
> What is the Day of noise and clamor?
> And what will explain to you what is the Day of noise and clamor?
> It is a Day whereon men will be like moths scattered about,
> And the mountains will be like carded wool.
> Then, he whose balance [of good deeds] will be found heavy,
> Will be in a life of good pleasure and satisfaction.
> But he whose balance [of good deeds] will be found light—
> Will have his home in a bottomless pit.
> And what will explain to you what this is?
> It is a fire blazing fiercely!
>
> (Chapter 101)

According to popular belief, the coming of doomsday is foretold by a number of signs similar to those found in the Book of Revelations: a struggle between good and evil, the changed rising of the sun, the sounding of a trumpet, and the appearance of a beast. When things reach their darkest point a messiah returns and gathers up all virtuous people to await doomsday and resurrection. It is important to note that, according to the Qur'an, the world does not so much come to a complete end as it is utterly transformed. It is therefore easy to argue that the afterlife occurs right here and not in some other place (in other words, Heaven is not necessarily somewhere above us).

After the end of the world, all human beings who have ever lived will be resurrected and judged. Some Muslims believe that this resurrection is only spiritual and that we will not be restored to our physical bodies. At judgment we will stand face to face with God for the first time and will be expected to answer for our actions. Those completely free from sin will go directly to Heaven. Others will have to spend time in Hell to pay for their sins before they enter Heaven to live eternally. Islam does not have a strong concept of eternal damnation in Hell; the time people spend there depends on the degree to which they have sinned. The only category of people who will stay in Hell forever are religious hypocrites, those who claim to be Muslims but are not. This kind of hypocrisy is regarded as such a great sin that no amount of punishment can adequately pay for it.

The Qur'an paints an extremely vivid picture of Heaven as a garden with streams and fruit trees, where we will live a lavish and comfortable life. Many Muslims take this picture of Heaven literally. Others see it as a metaphor for a state of spiritual bliss, where the greatest reward will be living closely with God.

Pillars of Practice

Paralleling the "Pillars of Faith" are certain ritual practices which are required of all pious Muslims. These are the **Shahada**, Prayer, Fasting, giving Charity, and the Hajj pilgrimage (many Muslims regard **Jihad**—striving in the path of God—as an unofficial sixth pillar). Even though they recognize the importance of these rituals, many Muslims do not observe all of them or observe them only partially. Islamic law provides extensive guidelines on the circumstances under which one is not obligated to engage in ritual and on how one makes up for ritual responsibilities that one has missed.

It is very important to make a formal intention to engage in a ritual before actually doing it, otherwise the ritual obligation will not have been fulfilled. For example, Muslims are obligated to donate a percentage of their wealth in a form of charity called *zakat*. If one were to give away money without first making the conscious intention of fulfilling one's *zakat* obligation, it would still be a good deed but would not count as *zakat*.

Shahada

Shahada literally means "witnessing" and is a shorter form of the term Kalimat al-shahada, the statement of bearing witness that forms the credal formula of Islam. The statement literally translates as: "I bear witness that there is no god except the God and I bear witness that Muhammad is the messenger of the God!"

This formula is often broken into its components in order to show what the central beliefs of Islam are, especially the nature of the Islamic understanding of God. The whole formula is framed as an avowal or assertion; in other words, it is supposed to be a voluntary and conscious declaration of one's beliefs. Uttering the first half of the Shahada makes one a monotheist but not necessarily a Muslim; it is something that could be said just as faithfully by Christians or Jews. The second half of the formula ("Muhammad is the messenger of the God") distinguishes Muslims from other monotheists, because belief in the finality of Muhammad's prophetic mission is what sets Muslims apart from followers of other religions.

The Shahada so perfectly encapsulates the essence of Islamic faith it is often referred to as the foundation stone on which the Pillars of Faith and Pillars of Practice stand. It is the first thing that is whispered into a baby's ears when she is born, and it is the utterance that Muslims try to have on their lips at the moment of death. It is also the formula by which one converts to Islam, such that many people believe that simply uttering the Shahada makes one a Muslim.

Prayer

Sunnis and Twelver Shi'is, who together account for the overwhelming majority of all Muslims, are ritually required to pray five times a day. This kind of prayer, called **Salat** in Arabic and **Namaz** in many other languages, is very formal and ritualistic, and is not to be confused with the informal, private prayer that most Muslims engage in anytime they feel like asking God for something or when simply conversing with Him.

Salat prayers are performed just before daybreak, just after the sun has reached the highest point in the sky, in the middle of the afternoon, just after sunset, and after dark. It is worth noting that although all the prayers are linked to the sun, none of them is performed precisely at the moment of a sun-related time (for example sunrise or sunset). This is consciously to disassociate Islam from any form of sun worship.

Muslims are not required to pray communally, although it is considered better to pray with other people when possible since this helps strengthen social bonds. One can pray at home or anywhere else as long as the place is not unclean. Cleanliness is more a matter of ritual purity than of hygiene, although an obviously filthy place (such as a sewer or public restroom) is not appropriate for prayer. Ritually impure places are normally associated with death, be it human or animal (for example a slaughterhouse).

Prayer is preceded by a ritual called **wudu** (or **wuzu**), which involves washing one's hands, face, and feet in a prescribed way. Once again, this is a ritual purification rather than a matter of hygiene. No soap is used, and when water is unavailable one can simply go through the motions of washing with one's dry hands. After entering such a state of ritual purity, the Muslim stands facing Mecca and makes the formal intention to pray. *Salat* prayers consist of a set of Qur'anic verses that are recited in a cycle of standing, sitting, and kneeling positions. Each cycle is called a *rakʿa*, the number of which varies according to which of the daily prayers is being performed.

One has little latitude in what one says during the *salat*; the majority of verses or phrases are set, being derived from the Qur'an. There are certain points in each *rakʿa* cycle when the individual Muslim can select a passage from the Qur'an to recite, but they cannot choose anything else to incorporate into their prayer (that is, a non-Qur'anic prayer or hymn). Furthermore, the *salat* prayers are always performed in Arabic, even by those Muslims (the majority of the population worldwide) who do not understand the language. As such, *salat* is not prayer in the sense of a personal conversation with God, but rather a ritual obligation which must be fulfilled to reaffirm one's relationship with God.

Fasting

Muslims are supposed to fast during the month of **Ramadan**, the ninth month of the Islamic lunar calendar. The fast consists of abstaining from eating, drinking, smoking, violence, and engaging in sex from before sunrise until after sunset for the entire month. Not only is one supposed

ART FOCUS

Prayer and the Mosque

PRAYER OCCUPIES A CENTRAL PLACE in Islamic religious life and ritual. The ritual prayer, called *salat* (*namaz* in most languages other than Arabic), is supposed to be performed five times a day, at set periods and in a prescribed manner. Although most Muslims do not observe this ritual with such regularity, they do consider *salat* to be a central aspect of their religion and associate its performance with piety. There are a variety of other forms of Muslim prayer, such as personal, informal prayers in which one asks something of God, or mystical prayers that help attain some sort of spiritual advancement. *Salat*'s status as a fundamental ritual sets it apart from these other forms and places it at the heart of Islamic religious life.

The Süleymaniye Mosque in Istanbul, Turkey, constructed in c. 1557. The small chimneys in the foreground belong to one of the schools that form part of the mosque complex.

During *salat* worshipers kneel and place their foreheads on the floor as a symbol of their total submission to the will of God (known as **sajda**, or prostration). Some people proudly bear a callous mark in the middle of their foreheads as a symbol of a lifetime of prayer. The *sajda*'s importance is obvious from the fact that an Islamic house of prayer (the equivalent of a church or synagogue) is called a **masjid**, or "place of doing the *sajda*." Through Spanish, *masjid* has made its way into English as the word "mosque."

Muslims are not required to go to the mosque in order to perform their ritual prayers but are encouraged to do so, particularly in the case of the midday prayer on Fridays (designated as the weekly congregational prayer) and for the special prayers offered on major religious holidays. Indeed, there are many Muslims who pray only on these occasions. Mosques vary tremendously in size, architectural style, and wealth of ornamentation; they can be as simple as a courtyard with a mark on the wall to indicate the direction of prayer (called the **qibla**), or imposing cathedral-like buildings that dominate a city's skyline and represent the pinnacle of architectural expertise in their society. Most commonly, mosques contain a source of water for people to perform their ablutions prior to prayer; a niche—called a **mihrab**—which marks the direction of the *qibla*; and a pulpit—called a **minbar**—which is used for sermons, lectures, and general announcements. *Minbars* can be fixed or movable and are frequently made of ornately carved wood or stone. The *mihrab* is an artistic focal point of the mosque; state- or imperially funded congregational mosques have stunning *mihrabs* of tilework or inlay of the most ornate kind.

The atmosphere in most mosques tends to be relaxed and informal. They contain no furniture (since Muslims pray on the ground) and, in societies relatively free of crime or sectarian violence, are kept unlocked. It is not uncommon to find people sitting in small groups inside a mosque engaging in informal prayers or casual conversation, or simply taking a break from the heat of the day or the crowded streets. Major mosques, such as the massive Süleymaniye Mosque in Istanbul, Turkey, serve as the focal point of entire towns or quarters of large cities. Built in the sixteenth century, it sits at the center of a large complex that included a hospital, public kitchens, an orphanage, and educational institutions, called **madrasas**, which taught religious and scientific studies. At a more abstract level, the complex symbolized an Islamic model of the world and the values that are considered important within it.[3]

to refrain from these things but also from thinking about them. Going
hungry and thirsty and avoiding violent or sexual thoughts is supposed
to teach one self-awareness, and also make one more sympathetic
toward those less fortunate than oneself—those who not only have to go
without food and water through necessity, but also have to hide their
anger and desire because they always live at the mercy of others.

Ramadan is the holiest month of the Islamic year, and fasting is one
of the most social of Islamic rituals. In countries with an Islamic majority the entire daily schedule changes during Ramadan to accommodate
the fast. Most families wake up before sunrise to eat a substantial break-
fast and to pray. The beginning of the fast is either announced by a siren
blast or else by men who walk through the streets beating a drum.
Restaurants either close completely during the day or else are very dis-
creet about serving customers. In some conservative societies it is ille-
gal to eat or drink in public, and only certain restaurants are allowed to
stay open in order to feed non-Muslims or travelers. Many Muslims break
the fast in a simple way by drinking water and eating either some salt or
else a few dates, in imitation of Muhammad's practice. Supper tends to
be more lavish than it would be at other times of the year. The entire
month has a festive atmosphere combined with a great sense of piety.
Children often insist on fasting, because the practice is associated with
growing up; the first time one is allowed by one's parents to fast for a
whole day or for the entire month is a major event in many Muslims'
lives and serves as an informal rite of passage.

Alms-giving

The giving of charity is considered an extremely meritorious act in Islam.
Just as in the case of prayer, a particular kind of alms-giving is differentiated from others because it is done ritually. Known as *zakat*, it consists
of giving away a certain percentage of one's wealth in charity. The percentage given away varies by sect, ranging from 2.5 percent among
Sunnis to 10 percent in some Shi'i groups. There is also a great deal of
variation in what forms of wealth and income are considered taxable for
zakat: for example, whether or not income (as opposed to assets) is taxable, and in how one calculates the tax for agricultural products.

In some modern Islamic societies the *zakat* tax is collected by the
government in the same way as other taxes. This tax income is used
exclusively for religious purposes or for social welfare, such as the building of hospitals or schools. In other societies people are responsible
themselves for making the charitable contributions to causes of their

choice. Some Muslims give the entire sum to their local mosque or to a respected religious leader, who applies it to good use. This practice is particularly common among Shi'is and is partly responsible for the greater social influence enjoyed by Shi'i clerical families when compared to their Sunni counterparts. Other Muslims divide the money and give some of it to charities and the rest directly to needy individuals. In the past, wealthy Muslims used their *zakat* to support poorer families, or destitute orphans, for the duration of the recipients' lives. Others endowed entire schools or hospitals and covered their expenses. Such uses of *zakat* have become uncommon in modern times, but they are not unheard of.

Hajj

Hajj is the name of the pilgrimage to Mecca, which all Muslims are supposed to perform once in their lives if they have the means to do so. The Hajj must be undertaken at a specific time of year, from the first few days of the pilgrimage month (the last month of the Islamic calendar, known as Dhu al-hijja) up to the tenth of the same month. If the pilgrimage to Mecca is carried out at some other time of year, and thus does not include an important set of rituals that take place at sacred sites outside the city, it is called an *umra*; it is still a good deed but does not fulfill a Muslim's duty to perform the Hajj.

For fourteen hundred years the Hajj has replayed the pilgrimage performed by Muhammad after Mecca had surrendered to the Muslims. Participants enter a state of ritual purity and wear a special pilgrim's dress before arriving in Mecca, and for the entire period of the Hajj abstain from paying attention to their appearance and toilet. They begin by walking seven times around the Ka'ba, the focal point of Islamic faith. The Ka'ba is a simple brick building believed to have been built by Abraham as a temple for God and now serves not only as the focus of the Hajj but also as the direction in which Muslims pray regardless of where in the world they may be.

After completing their circuits around the Ka'ba, the pilgrims run between two small hills named Safa and Marwa. This ritual recalls an episode in the life of Abraham and his family, in which Abraham had abandoned Hagar and her infant son Ishmael (Isma'il in Arabic) in the desert. When Ishmael cried out in thirst, Hagar ran seven times back and forth between Safa and Marwa looking for water. In the meantime, Ishmael is said to have kicked his heels into the sand, miraculously causing a spring to appear. This spring, called Zamzam, is believed to possess

spiritual powers, and pilgrims take its water as souvenirs at the comple-
tion of the Hajj. The water is frequently used for anointing bodies during funerary rites.

After completing the rounds between the two hills, the Hajj pilgrims then travel to two towns near Mecca to commemorate other
events in the life of Abraham. The last part of the Hajj involves spending
an afternoon in the plain of Arafat, where Muhammad delivered what
came to be called his Farewell Sermon. The Hajj comes to an end on the
third day, when the pilgrims sacrifice sheep and goats (and occasionally
bulls and camels) in memory of Abraham's willingness to sacrifice his
son and God's substitution of a ram in his stead (see p. 79). This sacrifice ends the Hajj and the pilgrims are free to resume their regular dress
and grooming.

Before the advent of air travel and modern shipping, the Hajj was
an arduous undertaking that required a great deal of preparation. The
slowness of the journey and dangers involved also meant that pilgrims

*At Arafat, Saudi Arabia, Muslim pilgrims from all over the world walk along
specially constructed concourses during Hajj.*

had to settle their affairs and make provisions for their families because of the genuine possibility that they might never return. For these reasons the departure of the Hajj caravans was a major event in all Islamic towns, and remains so to this day.

In modern times it takes a feat of organization to enable up to two million pilgrims to perform the same rituals in the same place over a few days. The Saudi Arabian government has invested large sums of money to create pedestrian highways, tunnels, and galleries to make the Hajj work as smoothly as possible. Jiddah airport, which serves Mecca, becomes one of the busiest in the world during the days immediately before and after the Hajj. Despite the best intentions of the authorities, accidents are not uncommon and overcrowding sometimes results in large numbers of casualties.

Jihad

Jihad, which stands for "striving in the path of God," is one of the most misinterpreted concepts in Islam. It covers all activities that either defend Islam or else further its cause. As such, wars in which Muslims tried to bring new lands under Islam were known as Jihad wars, and were understood and justified by Muslims in a way similar to that in which Christians understood the Crusades. In modern times any war that is viewed as a defense of one's own country, home, or community is called a Jihad. This understanding is very similar to what is called "just war" in Western society. In similar fashion, political extremists who believe their cause is just often refer to their guerrilla or terrorist wars as Jihad, even when the majority of their own society considers their acts to be completely unjustified.

For the majority of Muslims, Jihad warfare is almost the same as any just war would be to the average American Christian. Jihad theory allows a soldier to kill the enemy justifiably; without it he would be committing murder, which is a very grave sin in Islam. Similarly, someone who dies in the just cause of Jihad dies a martyr's death and is forgiven his or her sins.

Islamic scholars speak of an outer Jihad, which could be either Jihad of the Sword (such as the "just war" mentioned above), or Jihad of the Pen—engaging in written defenses of Islam, missionary activity, or simply furthering one's own education. However, there is also an inner Jihad—the battle all individuals wage against their own baser instincts. Because of its inherent difficulty, this is often called the Greater Jihad.

Observances: Life-cycle Rites

Islamic societies the world over practice a number of rites to mark each individual's path through life from birth to death. Most of these rites differ markedly in their details from one society to the next. There are, however, certain turning points in human life that are particularly emphasized as Islamic religious events and which, at some basic level, are observed in similar ways. Three of these life-cycle rites are the circumcision of male children, marriage, and death and funerary customs.

Circumcision

Male circumcision is not mentioned in the Qur'an but the practice is believed to be essential in all Islamic societies. Hadith describes it as a custom practiced by all prophets before Muhammad and particularly by Abraham, who is said to have circumcised himself at the age of eighty. Muslim boys are circumcised from early infancy until the onset of puberty, depending on the culture to which they belong and the social class of their parents. In many Islamic communities the ideal age is seven days, because tradition states that Muhammad performed the ritual on his grandchildren, Hasan and Husayn, when they were one week old. In other contexts the age is ten years, because another hadith says that the Prophet's cousin, Ibn Abbas, was circumcised at that age. For many urban families the rite is performed on an infant in a hospital or clinic and is accompanied by very little fanfare. For others it occurs as part of a major ceremony and is a rite of passage that is remembered by the boy on whom it is performed. This is particularly true of Malaysia and Turkey, where circumcision usually occurs around the age of thirteen. The boy is dressed as a prince and, depending on the financial means of the family, an elaborate feast takes place after the ceremony, at which time the boy receives a large number of gifts. In these societies the circumcision serves as a puberty rite that marks a boy's passage into adulthood. The public nature of the ceremony allows him to show his bravery and honor; after this ceremony he is considered a full member of Islamic society and is expected to pray and fast like an adult.

Marriage

Marriage is a basic component of Muslim social life, and though not explicitly listed as a religious duty, many people consider it as such and view a celibate or monastic life as somehow inferior and incomplete. Their justification for this view lies in the frequent references to marriage in the Qur'an as well as in the custom of the Prophet Muhammad, who was married himself. The Prophet reportedly said that there should be no celibacy in Islam, and that when a person gets married they fulfill half of their religious obligations. The Qur'an contains extensive rules concerning whom one is permitted to marry and what constitutes the rights and duties of a husband and wife. Details that are not found in the Qur'an are filled in from the *Sunna* of the Prophet and the living customs of each society.

Muhammad grew up in an extremely patriarchal society, where almost all economic and social power rested with men. The new Islamic laws of the Qur'an, by contrast, explicitly listed many new rights that women could demand of men. Muslim feminists and liberal theologians often agree that many of these rules seem archaic or unfair when viewed from the perspective of modern Western society. Yet it is important to note that they constituted important reforms in the legal status of women at that time.

According to Sunni Islamic law, a man can marry either a Muslim woman or one who belongs to another monotheistic religion. A woman, on the other hand, can only marry a Muslim man. This inequality derives from a viewpoint that sees the primary purpose for getting married as providing an appropriate environment for raising children. The patriarchal social system that has represented an ideal in most Islamic societies expects children to follow the religion of their father and expects the offspring of a Muslim mother and a non-Muslim father to be lost to the Muslim community. Shi'i law is even stricter on this issue and does not permit a Shi'i man to marry a non-Muslim woman.

Islamic law also permits a man to marry up to four wives at one time. However, the Qur'an encourages him to treat each of them perfectly equally and, in the very same chapter, states that this is impossible to do. Muslims opposed to polygamy see these verses of the Qur'an as an implicit outlawing of the practice, which, they believe, was only permitted as a temporary measure because pre-Islamic Arab men were used to having many wives and would not accept a sudden change in their marital customs.

The Qur'an stipulates categories of relatives referred to as *mahram* ("forbidden" or "sacrosanct"), who, by reason of particular degrees of affinity or blood, one cannot marry. In practical terms, the only difference with common Western practices is that it is permissible to marry one's first cousins. In many traditional societies this is the preferred form of marriage, because it not only reinforces family bonds but also makes sure that property remains within the extended family. In everyday life, the concept of *mahram* relationships is most relevant in communities and families where female veiling is prevalent, since women are not supposed to appear unveiled before a non-*mahram* male.

In its barest essence, the Islamic institution of marriage is a legal, contractual arrangement that provides a materially secure environment for children to grow up in and a socially acceptable outlet for sexual desire. The letter of the law sees marriage as nothing more than this and therefore concentrates on the details of entering into the contract and makes provisions for breaking it in the event of divorce. However, every Islamic culture attaches great importance to the marriage ceremony and buries the legal parts of the ceremony in an ornate series of celebrations. Many of these marriage customs are primarily cultural: a Syrian Muslim ceremony is very similar to a Syrian Christian one, just as an Indian Muslim wedding shares a great deal with a Hindu one.

The legal center of the Islamic marriage ceremony involves the signing and witnessing of the marriage contract. This contract can be signed either by the bride and groom or else by their guardians. An important aspect of the contract is the fixing of a "bride price," which is given by the groom to the bride and becomes her personal wealth. In some cultures the bride price is a promissory note, and serves as a strong disincentive for men to initiate divorce; in others it is considered little more than a formality or quaint custom. Nevertheless, the fact that it persists is seen by its critics as a glaring symbol of women's continued status as a commodity to be traded between men.

The Islamic laws concerning marriage allow for the possibility of divorce. It is legally easier for a husband to divorce his wife than the other way around, although there are clear provisions through which a woman can sue for divorce in the event of abuse, neglect, or abandonment. Nevertheless, most Islamic societies continue to be socially conservative and family-oriented, and even though divorce is legally permissible there is enormous social pressure against it. A very famous saying, attributed to the Prophet Muhammad, states that of all the things allowed by God the most distasteful is divorce.

Death
Muslims view death as the culmination of life, at which time human beings return to God and answer for their actions in this world. As a result, just as it is by members of many other religions, death is viewed by Muslims as a passage from one sort of life to the next.

Ideally, Muslims should die facing the direction of the Ka'ba in Mecca and with the *Shahada* ("There is no god but Allah and Muhammad is the messenger of Allah") on their lips. Those who are too weak to do so themselves are assisted by relatives, who recite the *Shahada* for them. In many societies people also recite the thirty-sixth chapter of the Qur'an, entitled Ya-Sin, which contains several powerful verses dealing with the subject of death.

A person is supposed to be buried within a day of their death: one who dies in the morning should be buried before nightfall, and one who dies in the evening should be buried the next morning. In practice, burials are often delayed by several days when, for example, an individual dies while away from home and has to be brought back for burial.

The corpse is ritually bathed before death, a task that is traditionally performed by family members who belong to the same sex as the deceased. This washing follows the same form as the ritual ablutions performed before prayer, except that the body is washed an odd number of times (usually three) using soap and water, which is sometimes perfumed. There is no tradition among Muslims of embalming, dressing, or adorning the body. The body is wrapped unclothed in a white cotton shroud, which covers it from head to toe. Coffins are not normally used but when they are, they are made of very simple materials.

The only acceptable way of disposing of a body in the eyes of most Muslims is through burial under ground. The grave is approximately five feet deep with an alcove carved out at the bottom (so that the grave has an L-shaped cross-section). The body is placed in this alcove resting on its right side with the head facing Mecca. The alcove is then closed up (sometimes with unfired clay bricks) and the grave filled in. Strict interpretations of Islamic law do not allow the construction of permanent graves; instead, they require graves to be simple mounds of dirt with perhaps a modest headstone marking the site. In practice, a long-standing tradition exists of making elaborate graves in all parts of the Islamic world, and some of the innumerable mausoleums of saints and aristocrats rank among the masterpieces of Islamic architecture. The Taj Mahal in Agra, India, is an example of such a tomb, as is the Mamluk necropolis in Cairo, Egypt. In some places entire cities have grown around the tomb of a highly respected religious person, such as those of Karbala in Iraq, Mashhad in Iran, and Mazar-e Sharif in Afghanistan.

Islamic burial is traditionally marked by a simple funeral service. Traditionally four men carry the funeral bier to the cemetery. The bier itself is usually a modest cot with a white or green sheet shrouding the body. Joining in a funeral procession is considered a collective duty: if there are not enough people accompanying the body to the cemetery individual Muslims are duty-bound to join in, although in the busy streets of modern cities the observance of this rule is increasingly rare.

The funeral prayer is a variation on the Muslim *salat* or ritual prayer, although the funerary service also includes several prayers for the deceased, asking for the person to be guided and forgiven in the afterlife. An interesting anomaly in Islamic rites concerning death and burial involves the treatment of children and martyrs: since small children are not believed to be accountable for their actions, the funeral prayer does not include a plea for forgiveness on their behalf. Similarly, martyrs are believed to be absolved of all sins; not only does one not ask for the forgiveness of their sins but they are also not bathed before burial, being buried in the clothes they were wearing when they died.

In many societies there are set days after the burial (especially the fortieth day) when special rituals are performed to remember the deceased. These normally involve the distribution of food or money among the needy and the gathering of mourners to read the Qur'an. Individual and collective wailing (especially by women) is also fairly common despite many injunctions against it in Islamic legal writings.

Observances: Festivals

All Islamic religious holidays follow the Islamic lunar calendar. Called the Hijri calendar in recognition of its origin with Muhammad's Hijra, or migration from Mecca to Medina, it follows the lunar year which is about eleven days shorter than the solar one. This means that Islamic holidays move backwards through the year, and festivals that are in the middle of summer one year are in the middle of winter a decade later. This prevents Islamic holidays from developing a seasonal character the way Christmas or Easter have.

Some of the holidays are official or central to the religion and are practiced either by all Muslims or, if they belong to a particular sect, by all members of that sect. Others, such as festivals of saints, are specific to a particular place. In addition to these holidays, Muslims also have seasonal holidays, which tend to be less religious in character. The best-known of these is the celebration of the Persian New Year, or Nowruz, coinciding with the spring (vernal) equinox and widely celebrated in Iran and its surrounding countries.

Eid al-Fitr: The Culmination of Ramadan

Eid al-Fitr (literally, "Festival of Breaking the Fast"; also called the "Sweet Festival" or the "Little Festival" in many societies) is celebrated on the first of Shawwal, the tenth month of the Islamic year. This holiday commemorates the end of the month-long period of fasting, which makes serious demands not only on the individuals who are forgoing food and drink but also on society in general, because the change in the eating schedule and the increase in the amount of time spent in prayer disrupts the rhythms of everyday life (one can argue that this is exactly what it is meant to do). The festival of Eid al-Fitr brings the changed rhythms of Ramadan to an end so that life can return to normal. In many ways Eid al-Fitr is the opposite of Ramadan. It is marked by a mid-morning communal prayer which is so well attended in many towns that the main mosques cannot hold the worshipers and prayer services have to be held in public places, such as fairgrounds and large squares. Whereas during the month of Ramadan fasting Muslims eat heavily in the early morning and at night, on Eid al-Fitr they normally do not eat regular meals but snack for the entire day. The atmosphere is festive: in most Islamic countries schools and offices are closed for two days and in some for longer; those who can afford to, wear new clothes, and children receive gifts from older relatives, most often in the form of money.

Eid al-Adha: The Culmination of Hajj

Eid al-Adha (literally "Festival of the Sacrifice," also called the "Major Festival") is the holiest of Islamic holidays and marks the culmination of the Hajj. This holiday falls on the tenth day of the final month of the Islamic calendar. The main feature of Eid al-Adha is the sacrifice of animals, commemorating the willingness of Abraham to sacrifice his son for the sake of God. In the Islamic version of this story (which is also found in the Bible), Abraham is asked by God to show his devotion by sacrificing the thing dearest to his heart. Realizing that this is his son Ishmael (Isma'il in Arabic), Abraham goes to him and tells him what has been demanded by God, to which Ishmael agrees without any hesitation. Abraham cannot bear to watch himself kill his own son, so he puts on a blindfold and goes through with the sacrifice by cutting Ishmael's throat. Upon removing the blindfold, Abraham is astonished to see Ishmael standing unharmed beside him and at his feet a dead ram that God substituted in Ishmael's stead.

Muslims who have the financial means are expected to sacrifice rams to commemorate this event. In some cultures people use other domesticated animals such as goats, cattle, or camels. The main requirement is that the animal be a completely healthy adult male. The flesh of the animal is divided between one's family, neighbors, and the poor. Since every pilgrim at the Hajj sacrifices an animal, the amount of meat at Mecca at this time far exceeds the ability of people to consume it. In order to prevent any wastage this meat is canned and used throughout the year by relief organizations. Many Muslims who live as minorities in western Europe or the United States find it difficult to fulfill their obligation in person and so patronize international organizations that perform the sacrifice on one's behalf, and distribute the meat among the needy in the country of one's choice.

Muharram

Muharram is the name of the first month of the Islamic calendar, and has become synonymous with a mourning ritual practiced by member of the Twelver Shi'i sect to commemorate the martyrdom of Muhammad's cousin Ali and, more importantly, Ali's son and Muhammad's grandson Husayn. Over the first ten days of the month people engage in a number of activities: every night, in front of tearful audiences, professional storytellers relate colorful and heart-rending tales of Husayn's martyrdom. There are also "Passion plays," called **ta'ziyas**, in which the ordeals of Husayn and his family are acted out. Audiences frequently get deeply involved in the play, and it is not uncommon for the actor playing the chief villain Shimr, who struck the blow that killed Husayn, to require a police escort to leave the theater.

The most distinctive Muharram ritual is the mourning procession, also called a **ta'ziya**. It has a few central objects: lights leading the procession, a float representing the coffin of Husayn, some sort of container for his weaponry, and a horse to stand in place of his mount. There is frequently also another float that carries little children dressed in traditional Arab clothes to depict those members of Husayn's family who were taken prisoner after his martyrdom. The procession is accompanied by celebrants, all of whom engage in some form of ritual mourning, including cutting oneself with knives and razor blades. Senior Shi'i clerics in all societies frown upon these violent mourning rituals and actively discourage the population from engaging in them, with only limited success.

Popular Holidays

In addition to the major religious holidays mentioned above, several other holidays are also celebrated in varying ways across the Islamic world. Some of these are regional or sectarian holidays, often consisting of festivals associated with a particular Sufi or Shiʿi shrine. Others are holidays commemorating events in the life of the Prophet: these include his birthday, celebrated on the 12th of Rabi al-Awwal (the third month); the Night of Ascension ("Laylat al-Miʿraj," or "Shab-e miʿraj," on the 27th of Rajab), when Muhammad is believed to have ascended to Heaven to converse with God; and the Night of Power ("Laylat al-Qadr," on the night between the 26th and 27th of Ramadan) which marks the anniversary of the first revelation of the Qurʾan to Muhammad. Many Muslims stay awake in prayer for this entire night, believing that requests made on this night will be granted by God.

The Islamic world continued to expand geographically, culturally, and politically throughout the centuries of Abbasid dominance and even after that empire's political decline in the twelfth and thirteenth centuries. The first half of the thirteenth century was a critical time in Islamic history because of the Mongol invasion, which spread across western Asia and culminated in the destruction of the imperial capital

Baghdad in 1258. Baghdad was the Rome of its day: it was the seat of the Abbasids, the central city of the Islamic world, and in many ways the most cosmopolitan city in the Mediterranean world. Its destruction and the accompanying subjugation of the important Islamic regions of Iran and Iraq to non-Muslim Mongol rule were a major crisis in Muslims' perception of themselves as God's favored religious community. This in turn created a theological trauma unmatched by any other until the advent of European colonialism.

Mongol rule proved to be extremely short-lived, but it heralded a new era in which cultural and political dominance in the Islamic world shifted away from Arabs toward Persians, Turks, and other ethnic groups. However, Arabic continued to be the language of most scholarship and also of communications between people from far-flung regions of the Islamic world. Throughout this period, missionaries, mystics, and merchants carried Islam further afield, so that by the sixteenth century it had become established in Indonesia, East Africa, and the grasslands south of the Sahara in West Africa.

Islam reached its maximum social and geographic expansion in the seventeenth century, at about the same time as Europe began to make rapid political and cultural gains. Many observers have seen a causal relationship between the declining power and importance of the Islamic world and the rise of Christian Europe. Muslim historical revisionists blame the shift in power on the intellectual stagnation of Muslim schol-

The Court of the Lions, The Alhambra, Granada, Spain, 1354–91. The Alhambra Palace complex (from the Arabic al-Hamra, "the red") is a remnant of the brilliant late flowering of Islamic culture in Spain that all but rivaled that of the Umayyad golden age some 300 years before.

ars, who are accused of ceasing to be intellectually innovative from as early as the thirteenth century, when there was a proverbial closing of the doors of *ijtihad* (independent reasoning). Europeans have wanted to see this as a result of the genius of their civilization as epitomized in the Renaissance and the Enlightenment. Apart from these broader societal changes, rapid technological advancements undoubtedly helped the West. For instance, superior naval technology enabled European nations to "discover" the Americas. It was not long before access to new sources of gold and trade propelled European development so swiftly that, in comparison, Islamic and Chinese cultures appeared to be standing still.

Islam in the Colonial Age

The encounter with Europe through colonialism and the unquestionable economic and military dominance of the world by the West in the post-colonial period have been critical in the development of Islam. With the exception of Turkey, Iran, Afghanistan, and Saudi Arabia, all Islamic countries were once under colonial rule. Even those that were not formally colonies did not escape the shadow of colonialism: Saudi Arabia, Iran, and Afghanistan were protectorates or else had to make substantial concessions in sovereignty to the British or the Russians; Turkey, the central province of the Ottoman Empire, was in constant contact with western European powers through its territories in Eastern Europe and North Africa, and had to make humiliating concessions to them in the nineteenth and early twentieth centuries. In more recent times the flow of technology and media from the West into the Islamic world has brought the Western world, its symbols, and its values, into virtually every Muslim home.

In the nineteenth century many Muslims acknowledged that the European world had attained a level of technology and scientific knowledge that far surpassed anything found in the Islamic world. Many members of the intellectual and political elite felt that the Islamic world needed to modernize its educational and state institutions in order to compete favorably with the West. The Ottoman Empire, in many ways the guardian of Islamic traditionalism, began a process of reform that eventually led to the emergence of Turkey as a secular republic. A ministry was established to administer religious endowments and trusts which previously had been independent. In 1868 the first European-style school opened in Istanbul and an Ottoman parliament was established in 1876.

The principal portion of the reform period, called the **Tanzimat** (1839–76), saw substantial changes in military training and organization, giving rise to a class of professional soldiers. They effectively took over control of the country in the early part of the twentieth century, thereby preventing Turkey's dismemberment after it lost the First World War (1914–18), and created a republic on ethnic nationalistic rather than religious lines. In the period from 1924 to 1928, the first president and hero of the republic, Kemal Atatürk, abolished the institution of the Caliphate, the Ministry of Religious Affairs and Endowments, and an entire educational system in which the religious officials were inseparable from functionaries of the state bureaucracy. He also abolished the religious courts and schools, banned all Sufi organizations, and ultimately declared that Islam was no longer the state religion. Two decades later religious freedoms were reintroduced by the government, but by this stage Turkey had already irreversibly separated religious institutions and functions from those of the state.

Tradition and Reform

Muslim thinkers of the eighteenth and nineteenth centuries have, for the most part, been preoccupied with the problem of strengthening and bettering their communities. Whether they see this as revitalization or simply vitalization depends on their view of the Islamic past and its relationship to the future. Some thinkers adopt a developmental view, which sees societal progress as contingent upon the adoption of a rationalistic, scientific worldview. Recent Muslim scholars, however, have tended to drop this model as too materialistic. In their opinion, it simply disregards the context in which development is supposed to occur.[1] They prefer to emphasize "authenticity," which better encapsulates societies' distinctive needs. In an Islamic context, authenticity can take one of two forms—individual authenticity, in which individual Muslims should seek to perfect themselves; and collective authenticity, wherein Muslims should strive to create a community that lives up to the full potential ordained for it by God.[2]

The notion of authenticity dominates much of Islamic thinking in this century, covering a spectrum ranging from extremely esoteric notions of individual perfection on the spiritual model to socially active movements that see Islamic authenticity as a society purged of all Western influences. In all cases, the quest for authenticity is based in a belief that there is an ideal form of Islam that is embodied either literally or metaphorically in the Qur'an and in the life of the Prophet. This "authentic" Islam is attainable and is the sole way of vitalizing Islam and individual Muslims.

Western commentators have labeled an entire spectrum of Islamic movements and individual figures as fundamentalist, and the term has attained wide currency in discussions about Islam in the contemporary world. There can be no doubt that there are Muslim fundamentalists, inasmuch as fundamentalism is defined as the belief in i) the inerrancy of scripture; ii) its literal truth and applicability across time and space; iii) the existence of an ideal form of the religion that would endure regardless of whether or not there were people actually practicing it at a specific point in time; and iv) the existence of an ideal or utopian religious community some time in the past.

But since belief in the Qur'an as God's literal and eternal word is central to Islam, one could argue that the majority of Muslims are, in fact, fundamentalists.[3] For this reason alone "fundamentalism" is not a satisfactory term to use in understanding categories of thought in the Islamic world. Yet other terms—reformism, revivalism, radicalism, and so on—are also not employed consistently, and can be equally misleading. In this chapter and the next one, I have used a simplified set of terms that derive from a conception of Islamic ideologies as possessing traditional versus modern images of the world, from varying understandings of the concept of authenticity, and from the nature of one's engagement with modernism.

Traditionalists are those Muslims who see a continuity in Islamic thought and culture from the Prophet's day forward, until the fabric of Islamic society was rent by European colonialism. They would like to see a return to pre-colonial times and the "authentic" Islamic society of that age, represented by traditional Islamic educational and social institutions, systems of government, and religious hierarchies. At its extreme, traditionalism rejects technological advances in their entirety, including electricity, modern medicine, and railroads (as was the case with the **Wahhabi** movement in Saudi Arabia in the early part of the twentieth century, although they have now come to accept technological development). Traditionalism is largely a defunct ideology, and is normally associated with aging religious scholars who see the modern world as undermining the privileges enjoyed by their profession.

Juxtaposed to traditionalists are not just **modernists**, but a much wider category of moderns. An important variety of moderns are the **Islamists**, individuals who believe in the necessity of establishing a society based on Islamic principles and governed by their own understanding of Islamic law and values. Most Islamists believe that by implementing Islamic law and "enjoining the good and forbidding the evil" they can convince the citizens of the state to adopt "authentic" Islamic values and practices, thereby creating an authentic Islamic society. It is essential to note that Islamists are not modernists, but they are certainly moderns in that they are conscious and active participants in the modern world, be it in the rapid social transformations that are occurring in the Muslim world through urbanization and migration, or in the use of the modern world's tools—ranging from the cars that have revolutionized transportation to the computers that have radically simplified information-sharing through print media and cyberspace.

Modernists, by contrast, subscribe to a spectrum of ideologies, all of which are united in their acknowledgment of a new significance to the nature of human life, characterized by particular forms of rational thinking and by a belief in the importance of the individual. They tend to share the belief that the processes leading up to the modern era involve a radical shift from traditional values, in which modern scientific and rational thinking replaces beliefs based on faith. In simplistic terms, Islamists embrace technology, modernists embrace the systems of values and thought that generate technology. Many Muslim modernists, particularly those from the end of the nineteenth and first half of the twentieth centuries, were deeply impressed by the accomplishments of modern science and held a deep optimism for the promises implicit within the scientific method. More recent modernists have, like many non-Muslim thinkers, developed a sober attitude toward industrial and capitalist development and their negative side-effects, and have embraced attitudes that center on individual rather than societal development.

Many Muslim modernists also embrace the ideology of **liberalism**, particularly in regard to the differentiation between opinion and truth, and the consequent belief that individuals holding different opinions can engage in debate. As a consequence of such debate one might be able to convince others of the value of one's own opinion, just as one might be convinced that the other's opinion is superior. As a matter of course, Islamists are not liberals, in that they do not allow for the possibility that there might be a difference between their personal idea of what is true, and what is actually true.

In the remainder of this chapter I provide short summaries of the most significant ideas of some of the most important Islamic thinkers of the late nineteenth and twentieth centuries. This is not intended as a comprehensive list, but one that is representative of a variety of Islamist and modernist thinking.

Early Reformists

Jamal al-Din Afghani

Jamal al-Din Afghani (1839–97) was concerned with two related causes: the defense of Islamic lands threatened by European expansionism and the internal strengthening of Islam. Often criticized for being overly political, this Iranian-born educator was in fact quite theoretical in his approach and has had enormous impact on two generations of Muslims.

Afghani rejected the prevalent notion that Europeans were somehow innately superior to Muslims. On the contrary, he argued, "authentic Islam" was itself ultimately founded on reason—the very basis of Western success. He accepted the validity of a scientific worldview and even declared: "The Islamic religion is the closest of religions to science and knowledge, and there is no incompatibility between [the two]."[4]

Islam had become weak and disunited because it had forgotten its roots and had tolerated centuries of unimaginative teaching and wasteful division. Combining older Qur'anic ideas of the *umma* (inclusive Muslim community) with contemporary nationalism, Afghani fostered a new notion of Pan-Islamism. He called on Shi'i and Sunni Muslims to reconcile their differences and present a united front against European encroachment.

Afghani echoed earlier liberal strands of Islamic thought, in saying that Qur'anic verses should be interpreted symbolically if they appeared obscure to modern eyes. However, in a radical break with the past, he decreed that anyone with a sound mind and familiarity with Muhammad's life could interpret the Qur'an. He believed that Islam's educational elite had a special responsibility to spread their knowledge to the rest of Muslim society, and he agitated against the existence of a clerical class of religious scholars. Above all, Muslims should strive to recapture the essential dynamic Islam of its golden age; if not, European powers would succeed in their ultimate goal (as he saw it) of obliterating Islam as a religion.

Muhammad Abduh

Following in the footsteps of Afghani, the Egyptian-born Muhammad Abduh (1849–1905) distinguished between the essential and immutable doctrines of Islam, and Islam's social and moral teachings, which should change when social circumstances change—albeit within principled Qur'anic restraints. Abduh championed sweeping reforms in Egyptian education, most notably in the emphasis given to the schooling of women. He failed to modernize Al-Azhar University, but he certainly did succeed in stimulating other thinkers. Some, like Ali Abd al-Raziq (1888–1966), discussed below, in effect accepted the need to separate religion from the state. Others, like the Syrian Rashid Rida (1865–1935), favored a rigorous defense of Islamic doctrines, and ended up supporting the strict Hanbali school of law, and eventually even the Wahhabi view of Islam.

Visionaries of Politics and Faith

Rifah al-Tahtawi

The Egyptian Rifah al-Tahtawi (1801–73) enjoyed something of a love affair with the West, but he also sought to redeem the best qualities of Islamic culture. Sent by Egypt's ruler, Muhammad Ali, to be imam to the Egyptian mission in Paris for five years, he wrote admiringly of French openness to new ideas. Back in Egypt, he modernized the country's educational system along European lines. At the same time, his own version of liberalism was very much founded in Islamic tradition. There was little difference, he argued, between Islamic law and European "natural law"; so in special circumstances Muslims could and should consult European legal codes if they could find the right answer there. Tahtawi also wrote with great pride in prose and verse about Egyptian history (including the pre-Islamic period) and is credited with giving a sophisticated intellectual foundation to contemporary Egyptian nationalism.

Ziya Gökalp

Although best-known as the ideological founder of modern Turkish nationalism, Ziya Gökalp (1875–1924) actually advocated a far more subtle blending of ethnic pride with a new concept of Islamic society. He believed that all societies progressed from the primitive to the organic and then to the modern—and that this was as true of Muslim states as of any others. Echoing Abduh, Gökalp spoke of two complementary but mutually exclusive historical sources: *nass* (text), consisting of the Qur'an and the authentic hadiths of Muhammad; and *urf* (social tradition), the behavior of a Muslim society, which varies according to context. The former is defined by God, and is thus not open to negotiation;

the second is a societal exercise, and therefore by definition malleable. Historically, he argued, all four main schools of Islamic legal theory have used different "recipes" combining *nass* and *urf* to arrive at new solutions to legal problems. Turning then to a more European formulation, he compared *nass* and *urf* with, respectively, the sacred and the profane. Divine text is sacred, but society's functionings are inevitably profane. With hindsight, even in classical Islamic times the sacred moral arena was differentiated from the profane political one. Gökalp concluded that the core of a religion could be separated from its societal interpretation. Put in terms of his own writing, he claimed that Muslims would not cease to be Muslims if they abandoned a defunct oriental civilization in favor of a vibrant, occidental one. In short, he accepted Western modes of rationality without rejecting Muslim values.

Ali Abd al-Raziq

The abolition of the caliphate in 1924 was a catastrophic event for traditionalist Muslims. For them, it symbolized not only a break with the historical continuity of the past, but a severing of the ties between Islam and political power. It was in this fraught atmosphere that Ali Abd al-Raziq (1888–1966) wrote *Islam and the Sources of Political Authority (al-Islam wa-usul al-hukm)*, a book that delved into Islamic history and Muslim sources to reveal a revolutionary conclusion: far from being a disaster, the end of the caliphate might mean a unique opportunity to separate (perhaps even to liberate) the world of politics from that of religion.

Brother of the rector of Al-Azhar and a student of Oxford, Abd al-Raziq certainly had the intellectual credentials to tackle such an issue. He argued that if caliphal authority derived from the Islamic community and not from God (as earlier scholars had suggested), then a change in the community's consensus (*ijma*) would obviate the need for a caliph. He hinted that even Muhammad's political office in society was distinct from his prophetic religious office, and concluded that the very notion of an "Islamic state" might be a contradiction in terms. Even if the whole world adopted Islam as its religion, for it to adopt one government "would almost exceed human nature and would not accord with the will of God ... The judgment of Allah is that mankind would remain diverse."[5] Islam, he declared, can never constitute the legitimate basis for a nation state.

Not surprisingly, traditionalist scholars criticized him for reducing Islam to a purely spiritual system. More seriously, they accused him of slandering the memory of the Prophet, and of calling into question the "ideal Islamic society." In response, Abd al-Raziq declared that an individual Muslim community was entitled to choose their own caliph if they wanted one. That meant that a corporate decision by any authentic Islamic society was itself by definition Islamic.

Muhammad Iqbal

Like Gökalp in Turkey, Muhammad Iqbal (1873–1939) is also widely known as the ideological father of a modern state (in his case, Pakistan). He first proposed a Muslim state in northwestern India as early as 1930, and was a much-loved national poet. However, his most lasting legacy may well be as a philosopher who regarded the kernel of Islam as being the betterment of the individual. Iqbal took the earlier Islamic modernist approach to science one crucial step further: for him, the study of nature was itself a religious act since natural laws were created by God. As he said: "Nature is to the Divine Self as character is to the human self ... [and] knowledge of Nature is the knowledge of God's behaviour."[6]

At the same time, Iqbal felt that the Qur'an pointed toward the spiritual nature of reality. In his view, religion provided answers to questions beyond the scope of science, which ultimately has only a "sectional view of Reality." Indeed, only religion enables human beings to understand their cosmic purpose, which is to be God's representatives in this world, despite all their failings. In this context, Iqbal interpreted the expulsion of Adam and Eve from heaven not as a fall, but as an elevation to another plane of consciousness. Adam—and by extension every human being—was a free agent, capable of disobedience and doubt.

Iqbal's worldview was a positive one. The universe was forever growing and improving, and humans would ultimately triumph over evil. But that required each and every individual to strive toward self-improvement, in the full knowledge that they bore responsibility for representing God in the universe. In many respects, these ideas reflected the prevalent attitude of European thinking, and indeed Iqbal enjoyed the benefits of a European education—first at a British missionary college in his native town, then at Government College, Lahore, and later at Cambridge, Heidelberg, and Munich. Yet his ideas also flowed directly from the Qur'an. The conclusions he drew, though, were revolutionary: self-perfection, in and of itself, becomes an act of prayer, and thus prayer need not be limited to Islamic ritual.

\ʿla Mawdudi

a Mawdudi (1903–79) was a compatriot and contempo-
ɪo took an interestingly different approach to the ques-
ɪd the state. While Iqbal hailed the imminent arrival of a
Pakistan, Mawdudi, an Islamic scholar and journalist, joined hands with
traditionalists to oppose it. In his view a national state was incompatible
with the belief that all Muslims formed one community (*umma*). He also
feared for the safety of the Muslim minority left behind in a Hindu-
majority India.

Nevertheless, when Pakistan was created in 1947, Mawdudi emigrated to the new state, where his **Jamaʿat-e Islami** organization agitated for a fully Islamist state. Two years before his death in 1979, Mawdudi
witnessed the promulgation of a system of Islamic law in Pakistan that
undid many "un-Islamic" civil rights and social policies.

Opponents considered Mawdudi an advocate of bygone ideas, but in
fact he was as critical of a petrified traditional Islam as he was of modern society on the Western model. He exhorted Muslims to aim for a
Prophetic socio-political order by reverting to "authentic" Islam, and to
jettison any practices that were not directly derived from the Qur'an and
Sunna. At the same time, he reinterpreted the concept of "caliphate"
(*khilafa*) to mean that each individual could now be a "caliph." In this,
his views resembled Iqbal's emphasis on self-perfection. But Mawdudi
saw the creation of virtuous individuals not as an end in itself, but as a
means of creating a perfect society. Echoing the Qur'anic decree,
"Enjoin the good and forbid the evil," Mawdudi firmly believed that the
authorities should enforce virtue within the community.

Sayyid Qutb

Sayyid Qutb (1906–66) has had probably the greatest impact of any
twentieth-century reformist thinker, particularly on politically active
Islamic groups within the Arab world. He became the leading ideologue
for the influential Sunni movement, the **Muslim Brotherhood**, and his
main work, *Milestones*, was adopted by radical groups—including those
who assassinated President Sadat of Egypt in 1981.

Qutb was influenced by Mawdudi and the Brotherhood's founder,
Hasan al-Banna, but he added his own innovatory arguments. Chief
among these was a radical reinterpretation of the concept of **Jahiliya**
(the Age of Ignorance). Traditionally, this denoted the shortcomings of
the godless and tyrannical pre-Islamic period. Yet Qutb extended its
meaning to apply to the corrupt leaders of nominally Muslim countries.

If society was not governed according to authentic Islamic principles, he argued, it would be incumbent upon all true Muslims to wage war against their "oppressive" rulers.

Followers interpreted Qutb's call in markedly different ways: some favored building schools and participating in national elections; others (a well-publicized minority) favored acts of violence and terror. In practice, the latter approach has flourished when authoritarian and non-participatory governments attempt to clamp down on opposition. In other words, oppression "radicalizes" otherwise moderate Islamists. Qutb himself was executed for his allegedly insurrectionary beliefs by Egypt's nationalist leader, Gamal Abdul Nasser. In a sense, Qutb provided a Sunni model for a mode of religio-political thought that became best-known in contemporary Shi'i Iran.

The Iranian Revolution

Twelver Shi'ism became the majority religion in Iran (classical Persia) from the 1600s, but this posed an ironic dilemma for its clerics. Historically, Shi'ism represented the oppressed, not the powerful; and doctrinally, Shi'ism considered that all governments would inevitably be corrupt until the hidden Imam returned to redeem humanity. Either way, politics was seen as a "dirty business," and political activism was thought to be futile.

Yet, equally logically, these same beliefs fostered a strong, independent religious hierarchy. In fact, this trend was accentuated in the eighteenth century, when a brief Sunni Afghan occupation of Iran forced Iranian Shi'i scholars to flee to Ottoman-ruled Iraq. There, in the cities of Najaf and Karbala, near the tombs of Ali and Husayn, senior clerics called **Ayatollahs** lived and studied. Even after Shi'is recovered the Iranian throne, most Ayatollahs remained in Iraq and continued to operate well beyond the reach of the Iranian state.

Taken together, these factors help to explain the ability of the Iranian *ulama* (religious scholars) to act independently of and in opposition to the monarchy during the nineteenth and twentieth centuries. A series of protests led to a constitutional revolution in Iran in 1906. As a consequence, a clause was added to the constitution the next year, stating that any law passed by the parliament would be subject to veto by a committee of five religious scholars, chosen by their peers, who would verify that proposed legislation was not in contradiction to Islam. However, the next year the king (called the "Shah"), drawing on the support of Russian troops, dissolved parliament and thereby suspended all the constitutional reforms that had occurred.

In 1921 a brigadier-general overthrew the ruling Iranian dynasty, and with the blessing of the traditionalist clergy, he crowned himself king in December 1925. In succeeding years, his artificially created Pahlavi dynasty (so named for its mythological pre-Islamic resonances) used the clergy as a foil against modernists, who demanded a more democratic system of government. The clerics disliked his pro-Western policies and monarchial pretensions, but acquiesced in the arrangement, preferring Pahlavi rule to the nightmare of a communist regime (a real fear, given the long border Iran shared with the Soviet Union).

However, by the 1960s Iran's human rights abuses and its overly conciliatory policies towards the United States led to anti-government demonstrations, involving both clerics and liberal elements. Ayatollah Khomeini emerged as the regime's most outspoken critic, and he was arrested after government forces attacked his seminary in Qom. Thousands died in rioting against his imprisonment. In 1964 an unrepentant Khomeini was exiled first to Iraq and then to France, from where he continued his campaign of denunciation. Finally, in 1978 a wide coalition of secularist and religious intellectuals, trade unionists, communists, and women's groups forced the Shah to leave Iran. But when clerics established a fully fledged "Islamic republic" in 1979, many participants in the struggle against the Shah felt cheated. Not only were they not represented in the new government, but the new regime employed the same security machinery and committed the same atrocities as the Shah did in order to silence all opposition.

Ayatollah Khomeini's career as the spiritual leader of Iran can easily be perceived in a negative light, since it was under his guidance that Iran became globally isolated, lost the trust of former allies in both the Islamic world and the West, fought a very costly war with Iraq, committed extensive human rights abuses within the country, undertook a policy of assassinating opposition figures living outside the country, witnessed the flight of many educated people and the loss of much of its wealth, and saw a decade-long period of economic stagnation. At the same time, many of the ideas Khomeini espoused before he became the leader of a revolutionary government are among the most compelling examples of radical Islamist writing and bear a striking resemblance to some of the concepts espoused by advocates of Liberation Theology in Latin America.

Ayatollah Khomeini

Khomeini (1902–89) claimed that it was the duty of religious scholars to bring about an Islamic state and to assume legislative, executive, and judicial positions within it. This particular form of government was to be referred to as "Rule of the Jurisprudent" (*velayat-e faqih*). The highest authority was to be a religious scholar who held absolute executive power, and who was qualified to hold this office on the basis of unrivaled knowledge of religious law. He was meant to have such a high level of moral excellence that he was, in fact, untainted by any major sin. There can be little doubt that when Ayatollah Khomeini took over as the religious leader of Iran after the Islamic Revolution he was ruling in precisely this capacity.

Khomeini based his ideas of governance by scholars on Islamic precedents, including the hadith which said: "The scholars of my community are like the prophets before me." Khomeini shared Mawdudi's idea of virtuous leadership creating a virtuous society. However, unlike most other Islamists of the twentieth century, he also stressed the symbolism of class and economic exploitation, which resonated with Marxist opponents of the Shah. As he put it: "If the *ulama* ... were to implement God's ordinances ... the people would no longer be hungry and wretched, and the laws of Islam would no longer be in abeyance."[7]

On occasion, Ayatollah Khomeini's exhortations in favor of the poor sound exactly like those of Roman Catholic liberation theologians writing in Latin America at the same time:

> Islam has solved the problem of poverty and inscribed it at the very top of its program: "*Sadaqat* [charity] is for the poor." Islam is aware that first, the conditions of the poor must be remedied.[8]

Ali Shariʿati

Some scholars have argued that Khomeini's conflation of traditional Islamic concern for the poor and the oppressed with Marxist and socialist ideas and symbols was a conscious attempt to capitalize on the enormous popularity of another important Iranian thinker, Ali Shariʿati (1933–77). Unlike Khomeini, Shariʿati did not belong to a clerical family although he had received a formal religious education alongside his regular schooling. After five years studying in Paris, Shariʿati returned to Iran, but his criticisms of the Shah resulted in his expulsion back to

France, where he died in what many regard as suspicious circumstances. Shari'ati lamented the fact that the best scholarship on Islam was conducted by Europeans and not by Muslims themselves. "As the followers of a great religion, [we must] learn and know Islam correctly and methodically. The mere holding of a belief is no virtue in itself," he said.[9]

Like Iqbal before him, Shari'ati exhorted his audience to become authentic by discovering their individual uniqueness. His works repeatedly explore this theme, using the example of Shi'i heroes like Fatima, Muhammad's daughter, who transcends her societal role to fulfill her destiny as a consummate human being.[10] Shari'ati saw the overarching message of Shi'i Islam as being a struggle to improve society through self-sacrifice. In this regard he quoted the example of Husayn, Fatima's son, who voluntarily accepted martyrdom in order to expose the criminal nature of his "evil enemies." Shari'ati wrote: "*Shahadat* (martyrdom) is an invitation to all generations, in all ages, if you cannot kill your oppressor, then die."[11] In Arabic the term *shahadat* connotes both martyrdom and bearing witness. What, then, is made of the person who commits *shahadat* but remains alive to bear witness? To Shari'ati, this sort of person—epitomized by Husayn's sister, Zaynab—had the special role of reminding the community of their individual and collective religious duties.

Conclusion

The thinkers presented here represent a variety of viewpoints that have proved influential in the last century. A clear progression can be traced from the early modernists such as Afghani and Abduh, both of whom saw in science and industrialization, and the worldview that accompanied them, great potential for strengthening Islamic societies in the future, to figures such as Iqbal, and on to Abd al-Raziq, who are progressively less dazzled by the dawn of the industrial age, and instead focus on various liberal values inherent in European modernism. Shari'ati represents a major step in the development of Islamic modernism, in that not only is he consciously introducing Western ideas into Islamic society, but he is also generating an Islamic modernity based on his own reading of Islamic history.

These thinkers stand in contrast to the Islamists, who actively agitate for an Islamic order enforced through the power of the state. As is apparent from both Mawdudi and Khomeini, several Islamists have been heavily influenced by the ideas of Muslim modernists, although they are selective in what they appropriate, and reject most liberal and pluralistic ideas. This trend has continued in recent times, breeding a high level of distrust between individuals who have differing ideas regarding the future of Islam and Muslims.

Looking to the Future 6

The desire to strengthen Islam from within and simultaneously to defend it from the perceived onslaught of the West has dominated much of Islamic thought in the last century, and has shaped the attitudes of a wide range of Islamic groups. Muslim reformers of many types, but particularly the Islamists, are trapped between two obstacles—not only do they feel threatened by the Western world, but they are also defeated by the rhetoric of their own history. Many Muslims remain acutely conscious of their glorious past, when the Islamic world was home to many of the world's richest cities and most important centers of learning. They find it impossible to reconcile their perception of their own destiny as a beacon to the rest of humanity with the fact that, at present, they are in no position to compete favorably with other, more vital societies, as well as with the bitter fact that not only is no Muslim country ranked among the most developed nations, but many of them are among the poorest and plagued with extreme social evils.

As outlined in the previous chapter, the majority of modern Muslim thinkers have argued that the best way to escape the present undesirable state is through a recommitment to an authentic form of Islam. However, in most quests for authenticity lurks a central, inherent problem: Whose authenticity is it?

> If women in Deh Koh, a village in the mountains of western Iran, have long put amulets on their babies to keep evil spirits away, does this not constitute an element of an authentic life-style? Do such women not have a right to be suspicious of religious militants who tell them that they should seek protections through prayer to God? The Islamic Republic of Iran has demonstrated hostility to this sort of

A Turkish postcard expressing sympathy for the victims of the civil war in Bosnia. The caption reads: "Blood, cruelty, and tears in Bosnia-Herzegovina."

"authentic" peasant behavior in the name of a revolution propelled in some considerable measure by appeals to "authentic" Iranian values against the godless, materialistic, scientific "universalism" of the West.[1]

The controversy over Salman Rushdie has served as both a weathervane and a lightning rod in assessing the relationship of the Muslim and Western worlds at the end of the twentieth century.

The Salman Rushdie Controversy

Salman Rushdie, an Indian-born Muslim, was already a well-established novelist in the English-speaking world when he released his *The Satanic Verses* in September 1986. Almost immediately the book sparked a scandal, caused not so much by its literary merit, but rather from the accusation that it lampooned the Prophet Muhammad, and thereby impugned the good name of Islam.

Much the strongest reaction came from India and Pakistan. The book was soon banned there, and fierce rioting broke out, followed by protests in Muslim communities in Britain, where Salman Rushdie himself lives. In California two bookstores which displayed the publication were firebombed. Most portentously, on February 14, 1989, Ayatollah Khomeini issued a personal legal judgment, or *fatwa*, calling Rushdie a "blasphemer," declaring that his crime was punishable by death and placing a bounty on his life. Ever since, the author has been forced into hiding in Britain.

The novel itself was written with Rushdie's characteristic combination of irreverent wit, satire, and a talent for creating a world of magic realism replete with multiple plotlines. Its title derives from a legend that verses 19 to 23 of Sura 53 in the Qur'an originally referred to three pre-Islamic deities as daughters of Allah. These purportedly false revelations became known as "the satanic verses." Furthermore, Rushdie offended many Muslims by suggesting that Muhammad's wives were prostitutes, and by writing a thinly veiled satire on Ayatollah Khomeini's life in Parisian exile.

The scandal led to a million hardcover copies being sold in its first year, mainly for its novelty value, making it probably the least-read bestseller of all time. But the repercussions of the Rushdie affair go far beyond the original issue of whether or not Rushdie's book was offensive. Most Muslims disapproved of the death threat on Rushdie, yet did not distance themselves from the protests. In a sense, the Rushdie affair illustrated a clash between two values: the right for an artist to express himself freely, versus the right of minority communities not to suffer abuse or discrimination for their beliefs. As the scholar Akbar S. Ahmed explained:

> If people in the West did not comprehend how dearly
> Muslims revere the Prophet, in their turn Muslims never
> appreciated the full impact in the West of their death
> threat to the author and the burning of his book. These
> actions have deep cultural meaning and resonate in history.
> They touch the rawest of nerves in the people of the
> Western world. Many of what they perceive as their grandest
> achievements and noblest ideas are involved. Ideally these
> include the principles of freedom of speech, expression and
> movement; of the abhorrence of censorship; of the respect
> for debate; of an open and free society ... The Inquisition,

the rejection of the established church leading to the
Reformation, Nazi and Soviet censorship—these are the
signposts on the road which they have travelled. For them
the image of burning books is one associated, for all time,
with the Nazis in Hitler's Germany. It symbolizes the
darkest of the forces of evil, anarchy and terror; it means
racial hatred and intellectual desolation.[2]

Nonetheless, the perceived "over-reaction" of a minority of
Muslims persuaded many in the West that all believing Muslims were
close-minded and violent. In point of fact, Shaykh al-Tantawi, Grand
Mufti of Egypt and arguably the supreme Sunni religious authority,
condemned the illegality of extra-judicial executions:

The best way to deal with this type of matter is to read the
book and reply to it scientifically so as to refute the errors
in it, unmask its author, and prove that he has unjustly
insulted God. As far as killing him is concerned, that is
inadmissible unless he is convicted of a crime punishable by
death. The execution of such a sentence is the
responsibility of the government concerned.[3]

Others noted that a Shi'i cleric like Khomeini had no jurisdiction over
Sunnis, and hence over the majority of Muslims in the world.
Nevertheless, in combination with other global events the Rushdie
affair did undeniably reinforce suspicions and stereotypes. The prevail-
ing Western reaction convinced many Muslims that the West was hos-
tile to Muslims, and doubted their full equality as citizens. They cited
the hypocrisy of British blasphemy law, which offers protection to the
Church of England but does not extend it to other communities.

By the same token, the affair illustrated the gap between working-
class Muslim immigrants to the West, who live in a communal cocoon,
and the better-assimilated intellectual class of Muslim citizen. The former group is not at all homogeneous, but its members tend to identify primarily with their ethnic and national group of origin, and cover a
spectrum from being completely unassimilated to integrating at work
but not at all socially. Many unassimilated immigrants harbor a distrust
for assimilated ones, because they see the latter as sellouts who are
betraying their cultures. In particular, individuals like Salman Rushdie
are seen as feeling a sense of inferiority relative to the Western world

which they can only satisfy by adopting an attitude of arrogant superiority to the average immigrant, whom they claim to represent, but with whom their contact is limited to those brief occasions when they visit ethnic neighborhoods in order to eat or to buy groceries.

Muslim Minorities in the West

There is, however, ample evidence that Muslims in the United States, Britain, France, and other countries are consciously mastering the symbols and tools of Western society (television and print media, and increasingly the Internet)—because they believe that these skills will both strengthen the Muslim community internally and help Muslims gain greater visibility and voice in the pluralistic societies in which they live as minorities. It is, in fact, largely through the efforts of such individuals, and not the assimilated elites, that Muslims have gained social recognition in Europe and North America. The Rushdie affair and some well-publicized instances of domestic violence in working-class Muslim communities in Britain have brought issues of Muslim and Asian immigration closer to the center of the national consciousness. At the same time as the British Home Office is warning that police attitudes toward the large community of Pakistani and Bangladeshi immigrants have created suspicion and hostility among these minorities and could lead to ethnic riots, in 1997 Britain elected its first Muslim Member of Parliament, and in 1998 the Ministry of Education approved two Islamic schools, one in London and the other in Birmingham, for inclusion among state-funded institutions. With this decision, Islamic religious schools and the education they impart are beginning to attain a status commensurate with that enjoyed by schools run by the Church of England, the Roman Catholic Church, and the Jewish community.

The case of the United States is somewhat different because of Islam's stature as an important religion among African Americans who are viewed as more "authentic" Americans than are members of the immigrant community. Islam came to the Americas with the first slaves brought over from West Africa. Though actively suppressed to the point of extinction under slavery, Islam gained a new symbolic importance in the United States during the Civil Rights era, when it was identified as authentically African, as distinct from Christianity, which was seen as a "White Religion."[4] Although early groups, such as the Moorish Science Temple and the Nation of Islam under Elijah Muhammad, were viewed as not quite Muslim by immigrants, under the leadership of Warith Deen Muhammad (and the posthumous charismatic influence of Malcolm X), the overwhelming majority of African-American Muslims have assimilated to Sunni Islam. Cooperation between African-American and immigrant Muslims—who together number approximately five million people—has resulted in a number of substantive changes for the betterment of Islam's status in the United States, particularly in the 1990s, when the U.S. President started issuing statements on major Islamic religious holidays, sessions of Congress were opened with Muslim prayers, and the U.S. military admitted Muslim chaplains. In 1998 Syracuse University became the first major American institution to close for an Islamic religious holiday—a landmark event that has not been widely noted as yet.

Islam in Context

A major tension within various Muslim communities is over who represents the normative form of Islam, and how (if at all) traditional Islamic practices, beliefs, and institutions should be modified to suit a rapidly changing world. Some modernist Muslims and Western critics tend to see traditional and Islamist interpretations of the religion as intolerant and as aggressive threats to the entire enterprise of human progress. They identify Islamic legal and ritual traditions with this contentious backwardness, and either reject Islam entirely or else search for some aspect of the religion that can be made to fit the perceived needs of the contemporary world.

Many commentators on Islam, both Muslim and non-Muslim, try to see in Sufi movements a more desirable and tolerant Islamic face. By contrast, Islamists and traditionalists are sometimes lumped together as undifferentiated conservatives. They are viewed as more concerned with conformity to outdated religious ritual and law than with the spiritual and physical welfare of individuals whom they force to conform to their own notions of acceptable social and religious behavior.

Commentators favoring the Sufi approach identify Islam's traditions of tolerance of behavior and belief as its most desirable feature. The most common barometers of this attitude are the positions concerning women's choices in dress and movement, and whether or not supposedly Islamic values are enforced across a society (for example restrictions being placed on the public consumption of food during the month of fasting, or on the sale and consumption of alcohol throughout the year). In fact, the correlation between social tolerance and Sufistic Islamic societies or systems of authority is not that simple. Many Islamic reformers specifically targeted problems within Sufism and successfully exploited negative public perceptions of aspects of Sufistic Islam in order to gain social influence.

Some of the Muslim attacks against Sufism and Sufistic society fit within the framework of the desire to promulgate an "authentic" form of Islam. In the opinion of many reformers, the majority of Sufi beliefs and practices did not exist at the time of Muhammad and are therefore undesirable innovations. Traditionalist Muslims not only criticize much of Sufi philosophy and many practices of meditation, but also the antinomian or heterodox expressions of Sufism, which are seen as morally degenerate and hedonistic. However, a much more potent critique of Sufistic society is based on the rigid and exploitative social system that allegiance to hereditary saints actually creates. In some regions of the Islamic world, such as among the Kurds of Turkey and Iraq, the Sindhis of Pakistan, and across parts of Morocco, political power rests with families of hereditary saints, who rely on their reputation as the possessors of *baraka* (which functions as a supernatural threat as much as it does a blessing) to ensure the loyalty of the local population.

Despite the potential for exploitation inherent in Sufistic social structures, in some parts of the Muslim world people identify Sufism as their genuine, indigenous form of Islam, as distinct from the imported, so-called normative tradition represented by the Islamists. This is particularly true in parts of the former Soviet Union, such as Chechnya, where the population has drawn a distinction between its own traditional form of Islam, which is based on Sufi orders closely tied to clan-based loyalties, and the Wahhabi reformism that is being spread by a network of missionaries allegedly subsidized by Saudi Arabia. The Wahhabis, who are easily identified by their voluntary adoption of beards, skullcaps, and veils, and their eschewal of tribal loyalties in favor of religious ones, have been subjected to ridicule and persecution, and occasionally thrown out of their ancestral villages. Wahhabis are seen as a threat to the traditional Chechen way of life and as the vanguard of a new, intolerant form of Islam such as the one enforced in Afghanistan.

Many critical universal issues influence this debate in Chechnya: the relationship between common people and elites, between Muslim societies and the West, and gender relationships and the role of women. Yet ultimately the central question is: Who can claim to embody "authentic" Islam?

Women in Islam

The Qur'an and Hadith literature make extensive references to the status of women, both in terms of their religious and spiritual rights and obligations, and concerning their role and status in society. The general thrust of the Qur'an appears to be to regularize the status of women, which varied enormously within a society of disparate tribal customs and economic conditions. Some members of pre-Islamic Arab society were so displeased with the birth of daughters that they killed them, a practice strongly condemned in the Qur'an:

> When news is brought to one of them, of [the birth of] a female child, his face darkens, and he is filled with inward grief! With shame does he hide himself from his people, because of the bad news he has had! Shall he retain her in contempt, or bury her in the dust? Ah! What an evil they decide on!
>
> (16:58–59)

Several other verses in the Qur'an clearly teach that men and women have equal religious rights and responsibilities:

> For Muslim men and women ... for men and women who humble themselves; for men and women who give in charity, for men and women who fast, for men and women who guard their chastity, and for men and women who engage much in God's praise, for them has God prepared forgiveness and great reward.
>
> (33:35)

Other verses imply biological equality between genders—"[God] created for you mates from among yourselves ... " (30:21). The Qur'an also stresses the importance of bonds of affection ("And he has put love and mercy between you" (30:35)) and mutual support ("Men and women are protectors, one of another" (9:71)). In other places in the Qur'an, however, men are clearly depicted as superior to women:

Men are the protectors and maintainers of women because
Allah has given the one more than the other, and because
they support them from their means. Therefore the
righteous women are devoutly obedient, and guard in [the
husband's] absence what God would have them guard. As to
those women on whose part you fear disloyalty and ill-
conduct, admonish them and banish them to beds apart,
and strike them. Then if they obey you, seek not a way
against them. Lo! God is most high, great.

(4:34)

Many Muslim feminists have argued that verses which endorse the
concept of male superiority were included in the Qur'an only because
the notion of women's inferiority was so deeply ingrained within Arab
society at that time. The more apologetic and polemical among them
argue that the Qur'an accords women much higher status than either
the Hebrew Bible or the New Testament or, for that matter, any Hindu
or Buddhist scriptural text.

Many Muslim feminists blame the patriarchal structure of most
Muslim societies on the environments in which Islam spread. In particular, they identify the Mediterranean world as one with a severely

*Young Muslim women grapple with computer studies in Malaysia. Most
Islamic countries are embracing new technology.*

misogynistic underpinning, one which was appropriated by Muslims as they spread into cultures that were materially much more advanced than the Arab one and were therefore seen as worthy of imitation. Even the historical development of the Hadith tradition is seen as illustrating this trend. Earlier collections relied heavily on information provided by Muhammad's widow, A'isha, and generally promoted equality between the genders. Later collections, however, played down A'isha's role and contained rulings that restrict women's freedoms.[5]

Despite the inegalitarian social structure that dominates the majority of Islamic societies, women from all backgrounds usually embrace rather than reject their religious tradition. Muslim feminists refuse to grant legitimacy either to Western critics who see Islam as inherently prejudiced against women, or to Muslim traditionalists who feel that a social structure in which women are subordinate to men is the only authentically Islamic one. They detect two competing understandings within Islam, one expressed in the pragmatic regulations for society, the other in the articulation of an ethical vision.

> The unmistakable presence of an ethical egalitarianism explains why Muslim women frequently insist, often inexplicably to non-Muslims, that Islam is not sexist. They hear and read in its sacred text, justly and legitimately, a different message from that heard by the makers and enforcers of orthodox, androcentric Islam.[6]

A further challenge to Western notions of emancipation (which are shared by many Muslim modernists) is posed by a tendency among young professional women to adopt the veil voluntarily as a symbol of their own empowerment. Such Islamist women see themselves as striving toward an ideal of authentic Islamic womanhood, and view other women who embrace Western standards of dress and appearance (and who are often the mothers of the newly veiled) as enslaved by value-systems that view women as ornaments and playthings.[7]

A Question of Interpretation

Central to most Muslim feminist positions, be they Islamists or modernists, is the belief that certain portions of the Qur'an, which seem to be unequivocal in stating that women are subservient to men, must be read metaphorically and seen as relevant only to the circumstances under which they were revealed.

In arguing for a contextual and metaphorical reading of the Qur'an, Muslim feminists are running counter to the widespread Muslim belief that the Qur'an is literally the word of God and therefore eternally binding in all contexts. However, they are by no means unique in distinguishing between the literal word of the text and its ethical vision. Many conservative Islamists and traditionalists routinely make such distinctions. A dramatic example is found in debates that occurred in the late 1970s in Pakistan over the religious legitimacy of that country's ban on slavery. Literalists argued that the Qur'anic verse which states that it is a virtuous act to free slaves means that slavery cannot be abolished, since to do so would be to deny future generations the opportunity to commit the virtuous deed of freeing slaves. This reading was resoundingly opposed by a broad spectrum of religious scholars, who read this verse in light of the Qur'an's ethical stand in favor of equality between human beings; they would see the verse as contextual, revealed at a time when Muslims owned slaves, moving them toward a time when they would no longer do so.

A similar tendency toward metaphorical interpretation is found in some Islamists' reading of the Qur'anic verse, cited above, which allows men to strike their wives. Apologists argue that the striking can be done with something as benign as a feather, stating unequivocally that physical abuse is contrary to Islamic values. Laudable as the desire to eliminate spousal abuse may be, such an interpretation in no way detracts from the fact that any instance that allows a husband to discipline his wife, but does not allow for the opposite, is incompatible with the notion of gender equality.⁵ The position does, however, transcend literalist interpretation, and thereby leaves the door open for future debates on the literal applicability of scripture.

Conclusion

It is impossible to predict the likely course of future events in all the varied societies that together comprise the Muslim world. However, it is safe to say that a major issue to be resolved in the first half of the twenty-first century is whether or not a plurality of understandings of Islam will be allowed to exist side by side in Islamic society. Liberal Muslim thinkers like the Algerian-born Mohammed Arkoun advocate a broader understanding of Islam, which encompasses all existing variations in belief and practice. Only in this way, he argues, can authentic Islam be realized.

Unfortunately, current social and political trends, not just in Muslim society but in the world at large, might suggest that liberalism and pluralism are in retreat, and that the future holds the prospect of greater conflict between disconsonant ideas of authentic Islam. There is a dilemma inherent in secular Islamic countries, such as Uzbekistan, Kazakhstan, and Turkey, which persecute Islamists and deny them rights of political and social expression. Such persecution backfires on the governments in question because it legitimizes the Islamists in the eyes of the populace and lends greater credibility to their allegations that the governments are corrupt and not interested in serving the needs of the people. On the other hand, the existing track record of Islamist groups in a number of societies should give no reason for optimism about their capacity to formulate more competent or ethical governments, or their commitment to preserve the civil and democratic political institutions that they exploit very skillfully in order to gain political power.

The identification in the public imagination of Islamists the world over with extremist groups such as the Taliban in Afghanistan or the Armed Islamic Group, which is held responsible for shocking atrocities in Algeria, weakens the Islamist position and encourages people to think more clearly about the difference between the Islam of their own contexts and the foreign Islam represented by the Islamists.

Perhaps the largest failing of many of the mainstream Islamists and some modernists is that they try and present Islam wholly rationally. Seen from such perspectives, Islam is the ideal religion because (they claim) it has the most efficient legal and social system, or because (in their opinions) it is in complete harmony with science, its truths confirmed by modern scientific discoveries. Such an understanding of Islam has virtually no appeal to the average Muslim—it is also potentially counterproductive because it ends up secularizing the religion by reducing it to nothing more than a legal and political system, albeit a perfect one. This robs it of any supernatural, sacred, or emotional dimension, precisely that aspect of the religion which inspires human beings not only to hold fast to the rope of faith but also to unfurl the sails of imagination and genius and produce those artistic and intellectual artifacts which are the essence of any civilization. In this respect, it is possible that the future of Islam lies in a renewed appreciation for and examination of its rich heritage, and an embracing of the various modern expressions of this vast and vibrant religion.

Notes

1 Islam in Everyday Life and Society

1   For more information on Muhammad, see Chapter Two.
2   John Renard, *Seven Doors to Islam* (California: University of California Press, 1977), 136.

2 The Birth of Islam

1   *Nahj al-balagha*, edited by Subhi al-Salih (Beirut: Dar al-Kutub al-Lubnani, 1983), 47.
2   An English translation of this sermon can be found in S. Mohammed Askari Jafery, trans., *Nahjul Balagha: Sermons, Letters and Sayings of Hazrat Ali* (Elmhurst, New York: Tahrike Tarsile Qur'an, 1978; rpt. 1981), 8–10.

3 Theology, Law, and Mysticism

1   Walter Andrews, Najaat Black, and Mehmet Kalpakli, editors and translators, *Ottoman Lyric Poetry: An Anthology* (Austin: University of Texas Press, 1997), 50.
2   For more information on the concept of the Evil Eye, see Clarence Maloney, editor, *The Evil Eye* (New York: Columbia University Press, 1976).

4 Beliefs, Rituals, and Practices

1   See Chapter 3, p. 47, for discussion of the issue of anthropomorphism in Islamic theology.
2   Much of the religious intolerance directed against the Ahmadiya is explainable by the antipathy large religious groups feel toward reform groups that emerge from within the larger body and seem actively interested in claiming converts from the larger sect. There is also a political dimension to the Sunni attitude toward the Ahmadiya, having to do with the self-identity of Pakistani Muslims and the construction of the Pakistani state. In this sense, the situation of the Ahmadiya parallels that of the Baha'is in Iran. For more information on the Ahmadiya and Baha'is, see volumes 1 and 2 of the *Encyclopedia of Religion*.
3   Gülrü Necipoğlu, "The Süleymaniye Complex in Istanbul: An Interpretation," in *Muqarnas* 3 (1985), pp. 92–117.

5 Islamic Thought in the Modern World

1   There is no end to the works dealing with development and the ideologies

accompanying it. A critical book in development of the ideology that developmental strategies should take into account the circumstances of particular societies was E.F. Schumacher's *Small is Beautiful: Economics as if People Mattered* (Oxford: Blond and Briggs, 1973). An influential work arguing against the idea that technology is free of cultural values is Arnold Pacey, *The Culture of Technology* (London: Blackwell, 1983).

2   For a detailed discussion of the concept of Islamic authenticity, see Robert D. Lee, *Overcoming Tradition and Modernity: The Search for Islamic Authenticity* (Boulder: Westview, 1997).

3   For a clear discussion of the phenomenon of fundamentalism in a variety of religions, see Bruce B. Lawrence, *Defenders of God: The Fundamentalist Revolt Against the Modern Age* (San Fransisco: Harper and Row, 1989).

4   Nikke R. Keddie, *An Islamic Response to Imperialism* (Berkeley: University of California Press, 2nd edition, 1983), 107.

5   Leonard Binder, *Islamic Liberalism: A Critique of Development Ideologies* (Chicago: University of Chicago Press, 1988), 142–3.

6   Muhammad Iqbal, *The Reconstruction of Religious Thought in Islam*, edited by M. Saeed Sheikh (Lahore: Institute of Islamic Culture, 2nd edition, 1989), 45.

7   Khomeini, *Islam and Revolution: Writings and Declarations of Imam Khomeini*, translated and annotated by Hamid Algar (Berkeley: Mizan Press, 1981), 123.

8   Khomeini, 120.

9   Ali Shari°ati, *On the Sociology of Islam*, translated by Hamid Algar (Berkeley: Mizan Press, 1979), 60.

10 Ali Shari°ati, *Fatima is Fatima*, translated by Laleh Bakhtiar (Tehran: The Shari°ati Foundation, n.d.).

11 Mehdi Abedi and Gary Legenhausen, editors, *Jihad and Shahadat: Struggle and Martyrdom in Islam* (Houston: IRIS, 1986), 214.

6 Looking to the Future

1   Lee, 178.

2   Akbar S. Ahmed, *Postmodernism and Islam: Predicament and Promise* (London: Routledge, 1992), 170-71.

3   Quoted in Anouar Abdallah et al., *Pour Rushdie: cent intellectuels arabes et musulmans pour la liberté d'expression* (Paris: La Découverte, 1993), 287. The translation is by Roger Allen in his review of the English language edition of the book (*Iranian Studies* 28:3–4 (1995), 231–3).

4   For more on Islam among African Americans, see Allan D. Austin, *African Muslims in Antebellum America: Transatlantic Stories and Spiritual Struggles* (New York: Routledge, 1997) and Richard B. Turner, *Islam in the African-American Experience* (Bloomington: Indiana University Press, 1997).

5   For more on the feminist reinterpretation of early Islamic society, see Fatima Mernissi, *The Veil and the Male Elite: A Feminist Interpretation of Women's Rights in Islam*, trans. Mary Jo Lakeland (Reading, Mass.:

Addison-Wesley, 1991). An account of how the image of Muhammad's wife, A'isha, changed over time to reflect changing notions of the ideal woman, see Denise A. Spellberg, *Politics, Gender and the Islamic Past: The Legacy of 'A'isha bint Abi Bakr* (New York: Columbia University Press, 1994).

6 Leila Ahmed, *Women and Gender in Islam: Historical Roots of a Modern Debate* (New Haven: Yale University Press, 1992), 65–6.

7 For more on the movement toward adopting the veil, see Sherifa Zuhur, *Revealing Reveiling: Islamist Gender Ideology in Contemporary Egypt* (Albany: State University of New York Press, 1992).

8 For more information on women's rights in marriage, see Chapter 4, pages 75–6.

Glossary

Abbasids The name of the **Sunni** dynasty that ruled much of the Islamic world through what has come to be called the Golden Age of Islam.

Abdallah The name of **Muhammad**'s father.

Abd al-
Muttalib The name of **Muhammad**'s paternal grandfather.

Abu Bakr Muhammad's friend, advisor, father of his wife **A'isha**, and the first **Caliph** of the **Sunnis**.

Abu Talib The name of **Muhammad**'s paternal uncle, who took over his guardianship after he had been orphaned.

adhan The Islamic call to prayer, which is broadcast from **mosques** five
(or azan) times a day.

Ahmadiya The followers of the religious reformer Mirza Ghulam Ahmad Qadian (d. 1908), who are considered apostates by many **Sunnis** because they grant him the status of prophethood.

A'isha The name of **Abu Bakr**'s daughter and wife of **Muhammad**; she outlived him by several decades and is one of the most important sources of doctrinal and historical information in the formative period of Islam.

al-Ash'ari The name of the most famous theologian in the history of Islam, and founder of the **Ash'ariya** school of theology.

al-Azhar The name of the most prestigious center of **Sunni** learning and one of the world's oldest surviving universities. It is located in Cairo.

Ali Muhammad's cousin and son-in-law; considered the first **Imam** by **Shi'i** Muslims and the fourth **Caliph** by **Sunnis**. He is one of the most important figures in early Islam.

Allah Literally, "the god," the proper name of God in Islam.

Amina The name of **Muhammad**'s mother.

Ash'ariya The name of the most influential school of theology in Islam.

aya Literally, "signs of God"; the term used for individual
(pl. ayat) verses of the **Qur'an**.

Ayatollah High-ranking members of the **Twelver Shi'i** clergy, who are authorized to engage in **ijtihad**.

azan See **adhan**.

baraka (sometimes **barkat** or **bereket**) A miraculous power bestowed on human beings by God, and believed to be possessed by **Sufi** saints.

batin A term used in **Sufism** and esoteric **Shi'i** thought for the outer, obvious meaning of a text, particularly the **Qur'an**.

Caliphs The leaders of the Muslim community after Muhammad. It comes from the Arabic word **khalifa**, which means "representative" or "delegate," implying that the Caliphs did not rule on their own authority but only as the representatives of God and His Prophet.

Chishti The name of a **Sufi** order that is extremely popular in South Asia.

dhikr Literally "repetition," "remembrance," "utterance," or
(or zikr) "mentioning," the commonest term used for **Sufi** meditational exercises.

Eid al-Adha The "Festival of the Sacrifice" that marks the end of the **Hajj** pilgrimage.

Eid al-Fitr The festival that commemorates the end of the fast of **Ramadan**.

fana A **Sufi** mystical concept that signifies the annihilation of a person's individuality in the oneness of God.

faqih A scholar who engages in the theoretical study of Islamic jurisprudence (**fiqh**).

Fatima Muhammad's daughter, wife of **Ali** and mother of **Husayn**. She is a focus of devotion in **Shi'i** Islam.

fatwa A legal opinion or decree; the answer given by a **mufti** to a question posed to him.

fiqh Islamic jurisprudence.

Hadith Traditions or anecdotes concerning the life and sayings of the Prophet **Muhammad**; used as a scriptural source of secondary importance to the **Qur'an**.

hafiz Literally, "guardian," an honorific title used for someone who knows the **Qur'an** by heart.

Hajj A pilgrimage to the **Ka'ba** in Mecca, which constitutes one of the ritual obligations of Islam.

Hanafi Name of one of the four Sunni legal schools.

Hanbali Name of one of the four Sunni legal schools.

Hashim The name of **Muhammad**'s clan.

Hijra The migration of **Muhammad** and his followers from Mecca to Medina in 622, which marks the beginning of the Islamic Hijri calendar.

Husayn The younger son of **Ali** and **Fatima**, and grandson of the Prophet. His martyrdom at Karbala is a major focus of **Shi'i** belief and ritual.

ijtihad The independent reasoning of a qualified Islamic legal scholar, referred to as a **mujtahid** or **faqih**.

Imam Literally, "leader," it is a term used for anyone who leads prayers in a **mosque**. More importantly, it is the title of the rightful leader of the Muslim community in the **Shi'i** sect.

iman Faith.

Islam Literally, "surrender" or "submission," the name of a monotheistic religion closely related to Judaism and Christianity; people belonging to this religion are called **Muslims**.

Islamists Individuals who believe in the necessity of establishing a society based on Islamic principles and governed by their own understanding of Islamic law and values.

Isma'ilis The name of a **Shi'i** sect.

isnad The chain of transmitting authorities of a **Hadith** account.

Jabriya An early theological school that maintained that humans act entirely by divine compulsion and have absolutely no free will.

Jaʿfar al-Sadiq The sixth **Imam** of the **Shiʿis**, who is credited with founding the principal school of Shiʿi law.

jahiliya Literally, "ignorance," a term used to describe Arab society before the advent of Islam. Certain **Islamist** organizations have started using the term to indicate all parts of the world that do not meet their standards of virtue and good government.

Jamaʿat-e Islami The most powerful **Islamist** organization among the Muslims of South Asia, with strong ties to Sunni Islamist organizations all over the world and growing influence in Central Asia.

Jihad The term literally means "striving" and is a shortened version of a longer name that means "striving in the path of God." The concept of *jihad* covers all activities that either defend Islam or else further its cause.

jinn Sentient beings mentioned in the Qur'an, frequently identified as demons.

Kaʿba A cubic building located in Mecca, believed to have been built by Abraham at God's command. It is the direction in which Muslims pray and the focus of the ritual pilgrimage called the **Hajj**.

Kalam Literally, "speech" or "dialectic," the commonest name given to theology in Islam.

Khadija The name of the Prophet's first wife, who is also honored as the first convert to Islam.

Khalifa See **Caliph**.

Koran See **Qur'an**.

liberalism An ideology that emphasizes, among other things, the difference between opinion and truth; it is based on the belief that people or groups with differing views should engage each other in dialog rather than try to prevail over weaker ones through violent or oppressive means.

Maliki Name of one of the four Sunni legal schools.

masjid A Muslim place of prayer; same as a **mosque**.

Mevlevi The name of a **Sufi** order that is limited to Turkey and some other areas that once belonged to the Ottoman Empire. Famous for its distinctive **dhikr** ritual called **sema**.

mihrab A prayer niche in a **mosque** that marks the **qibla**, or direction of prayer.

minbar A pulpit, one of the most important architectural features of a **mosque**.

modernists Reformists who subscribe to a spectrum of ideologies, all of which are united in their acknowledgment that the modern significances of human life are substantially different from those that came before it. Modernism is characterized by particular forms of rational thinking and by the belief in the importance of the individual.

mosque A Muslim place of prayer; same as a **masjid**.

mufti   Someone normally appointed by the government for the specific purpose of answering questions concerning the Islamic law (**shari'a**).

Muhammad The primary prophet of Islam, believed by Muslims to have received divine revelation in the form of the **Qur'an**, and to be the last in a series of prophets beginning with Adam and including all the prophets mentioned in the Hebrew Bible, as well as Jesus.

Muharram The name of the first month of the Islamic calendar, synonymous with a mourning ritual practiced by members of the **Twelver Shi'i** sect to commemorate the martyrdom of **Muhammad**'s cousin Ali and, more importantly, Ali's son and **Muhammad**'s grandson **Husayn**.

mujtahid A respected and learned Muslim scholar who has the right to engage in independent reasoning, or **ijtihad**.

Muslim   (fem. **Muslima**) A person who professes the religion of **Islam**.

Muslim Brother-hood (**Al-Ikhwan al-muslimin**) The most powerful **Islamist** organization in the Arab world, with strong ties to **Sunni** Islamist organizations in other Muslim societies.

Mu'tazila The name of one of the most important and influential theological schools in the history of Islam.

nabi   (pl. **anbiya**) A prophet. Belief in prophecy is an important tenet of Muslim belief.

namaz   The name of the Islamic ritual prayer; the same as **salat**.

Qadariya An early Islamic theological school that believed in absolute human free will.

qadi   An Islamic judge.

qawwali   A very distinctive form of singing practiced by members of the **Chishti Sufi** order as part of their **dhikr** exercises.

qibla   The direction of Muslim prayer, which is supposed to be performed facing the **Ka'ba** in Mecca from all points in the world.

Qur'an   The Muslim scripture, which is believed to have been revealed by God to the Prophet **Muhammad**.

Quraysh The name of **Muhammad**'s tribe.

Ramadan The ninth month of the Islamic lunar calendar, during which practicing Muslims fast, abstaining from eating, drinking, smoking, violence, and sex from before sunrise until after sunset for the entire month.

rasul (pl. **rusul**) A special category of prophet (**nabi**), whom God has given a concrete message, normally a revealed scripture, to be delivered to human beings.

sajda   The bowing-down or prostration that is one of the most distinctive aspects of Islamic ritual prayer or **salat**.

salat   The name of the Islamic ritual prayer; the same as **namaz**.

sema   A very distinctive whirling dance performed by members of the **Mevlevi Sufi** order as part of their **dhikr** exercises.

Shafi'i   Name of one of the four Sunni legal schools.

Shahada The Islamic profession of faith: "I bear witness that there is no god except the God and I bear witness that Muhammad is the messenger of the God!"

Shariʿa	Islamic law.
Shiʿah	Same as **Shiʿi**.
Shiʿi	The name given to a number of Muslim sects, all of which separated from the **Sunni** Muslim majority over the status of **Ali** as the successor to **Muhammad**.
Shiʿite	Same as **Shiʿi**.
Sufism	The name given to a wide range of expressions of mystical religiosity in Islam. The same as **tasawwuf**.
Sunna	The custom or tradition of the Prophet **Muhammad**, which is used as a source of law and as an informal model of behavior in everyday life.
Sunni	The name of the majority sect in Islam.
sura	The term used for individual chapters of the **Qur'an**.
Tanzimat	A period of modernizing reforms carried out in the Ottoman Empire, lasting from 1839 until 1876.
tariqas	**Sufi** orders, which have been very important in the history of Islamic thought and society.
tasawwuf	The name given to a wide range of expressions of mystical religiosity in Islam. The same as **Sufism**.
tawhid	The concept of divine unity, which is central to Muslim belief.
taʿwidh	Talismans that are frequently worn in many parts of the Islamic world to guard against the evil eye.
taʿziya	Passion plays by which **Twelver Shiʿis** commemorate the martyrdom of **Husayn** in the month of **Muharram**. The term is also used for mourning processions that are organized during this month.
tradition-alists	Those Muslims who see a continuity in Islamic thought and culture from the Prophet's day forward, until the fabric of Islamic society was rent by European colonialism, and who would like to see a return to pre-colonial times.
Twelver Shiʿis	The name of an important **Shiʿi** sect, which is dominant in Iran.
ulama (sing. **alim**)	The class of Muslim religious scholars.
Umayyads	The first dynasty to rule the Islamic world.
umma (**ummat**)	Means "nation" or "community" and refers to the community of believers made up by all the Muslims of the world.
umra	A pilgrimage to the **Kaʿba** in Mecca that is carried out at any time of the year except that of the ritually obligatory **Hajj**. The *umra* is considered inferior to the Hajj, but still carries religious merit.
usul al-fiqh	The principles of Islamic jurisprudence, which are used to interpret Islamic law (shariʿa).
Wahhabism	A **traditionalist** Islamic movement, concentrated in Saudi Arabia, which sees modern technological and social innovations as corrupt and agitates for a return to a Muslim society similar to the one in the days of the Prophet.
wudu	The ritual washing that precedes prayers (salat).

(or **wuzu**)

zahir	A term used in **Sufism** and esoteric **Shi'i** thought for the inner, hidden meaning of a text, particularly the **Qur'an**.
zakat	Ritual alms-giving, which consists of giving a fixed percentage of one's wealth in charity every year.
Zaydis	The name of a **Shi'i** sect, which is largely limited to Yemen.
zikr	Same as **dhikr**.

Holy Days and Festivals

Ashura (10th of Muharram, the first month): The Muslim Day of Atonement, marked by Sunnis with a voluntary fast. It is also the most important Shi'i holy day, commemorating the martyrdom of Husayn, grandson of the Prophet.

Eid milad al-nabi (12th of Rabi al-awwal, the third month): Commemoration of the birthday of the Prophet.

Laylat al-mi'raj (27th of Rajab, the seventh month): Commemorates Muhammad's ascension to Heaven. Also called **Shab-e mi'raj** and **Miraj ģejesi** in Asian non-Arab societies.

Laylat al-bara'a (14th night of Sha'ban, the eight month): The night on which every human being's fortune for the coming year is popularly believed to be registered in Heaven. It is marked both by prayer vigils and by feasting and illumination. In South and Southeast Asia it is also the Muslim day of the dead, when oblations are made in the name of deceased ancestors. It is also the birthday eve of the twelfth Imam of the Twelver Shi'is. Also called **Shab-e barat**.

Ramadan: The name of the ninth month of the Islamic calendar, marked by a month-long fast that starts before sunrise and ends after sunset each day.

Laylat al qadr (night between the 26th and 27th of Ramadan, the ninth month). The Night of Power. Anniversary of the night that the Qur'an was first revealed to Muhammad. Tradition holds that requests made to God during this night are granted. Also called **Shab-e qadr** and **Kadar ģejesi** in Asian non-Arab societies.

Eid al-Fitr (1st of Shawwal, the tenth month): The feast marking the end of the fast of Ramadan. The second most celebrated holiday of the Islamic year, marked by much festivity. Also called the Lesser Eid and the Sugar Eid.

Hajj (7th–10th of Dhu al-hijja, the twelfth month): The obligatory ritual pilgrimage to Mecca and its environs, which forms one of the Pillars of Practice in Islam. Only pilgrims participate directly in these holy days.

Eid al-Adha (10th of Dhu al-hijja, the twelfth month): Commemoration of Abraham's sacrifice of his son Ishmael (Isma'il in Arabic), which constitutes the culmination of the Hajj. It is the most important holiday of the Islamic calendar. Also called the Big Eid and the Eid of the Sacrifice.

Pronunciation Guide

This guide gives an accepted pronunciation as simply as possible. Syllables are separated by a space and those that are stressed are printed in italics. Letters are pronounced in the usual manner for English unless they are clarified in the following list. (The symbol ʿ indicates the Arabic letter "ayn," which is best pronounced in English by lengthening the preceding vowel.)

a	fl*a*t	o	n*o*t
ah	f*a*ther	oo	f*oo*d
ay	p*ay*	ōō	f*oo*t
ee	s*ee*	ow	h*ow*
e	l*e*t	u	b*u*t
ī	h*igh*	ā	*a*bout (unaccented vowel)
i	p*i*ty	izm	trib*alism*
ō	n*o*	j	*j*et

Abbasids: ā *ba* sidz
Abu Bakr: a boo *bak* ār
Allah: *al* lah
Ash'ari: *ash* a ree
Aya: *a* ya
Ayatollah: *a* yat ol lah
Baraka: ba ra ka
Caliphs: *kay* lifs
Dhikr: *dhi* kăr
Faqih: fa *kee*
Fatwa: *fat* wă
Fiqh: fik
Hadith: ha *deeth*
Hajj: haj
Hijra: *hij* rā
Imam: i *mahm*
iman: ee *mahn*
Ismaʿilis: is *mah* ee leez
Jihad: ji *hahd*
Kaʿba: *kah* ba
Kalam: ka *lahm*
Khalifa: ka *lee* fa
Masjid: *mas* jid
Mihrab: *me* rahb
Muhammad: mōō *ham* mad

Muharram: mōō *har* ram
Muʿtazila: mōō *ta* zi lă
Nabi: *na* bee
Namaz: na *mahz*
Qadi: *kah* dee
Qibla: *kib* lă
Qur'an: kōr *an*
Quraysh: ku *raysh*
Sajda: *saj* dă
Salat: să *laht*
Sema: se mah
Shahada: sha *hah* da
Shariʿa: sha *ree* ah
Shiʿi (Shi'ite): *shee* ee
Sufism: soo fee izm
Sunna: *sōōn* na
Sunni: *sōōn* nee
Sura: soo *rā*
Tawhid: tow *heed*
Taʿwidh: tah *weedh*
Ulama: oo la mah
Umayyads: o *may* yadz
Umma: *ōōm* mă
Umra: *ōōm* rā
Wudu: wu *doo*

Suggested Further Reading

ERVAND ABRAHAMIAN, *Khomeinism: Essays on the Islamic Republic* (Berkeley: University of California Press, 1993)

A book explaining how the charisma of Khomeini came to dominate Iran after the revolution, and outlining the use of non-Islamic symbolism in sustaining the revolution.

MAHNAZ AFKHAMI (ed.), *Faith and Freedom: Women's Human Rights in the Muslim World* (Syracuse: Syracuse University Press, 1995)

An important and critically written collection of essays on problems facing women in a wide variety of Islamic contexts.

LEILA AHMED, *Women and Gender in Islam: Historical Roots of a Modern Debate* (New Haven: Yale University Press, 1992)

A very readable survey book on issues of gender and religion in Islam.

MOHAMMED ARKOUN, *Rethinking Islam: Common Questions, Uncommon Answers.* Trans. Robert D. Lee (Boulder: Westview Press, 1994)

Writings of an important modern Muslim thinker known for his liberal and pluralistic conception of Islam.

ALLAN D. AUSTIN, *African Muslims in Antebellum America: Transatlantic Stories and Spiritual Struggles* (New York: Routledge, 1997)

Captivating stories of the lives of sub-Saharan Africans brought to the Americas as slaves.

STEVEN BARBOZA (ed.), *American Jihad: Islam After Malcolm X* (New York: Doubleday, 1993)

A collection of short and engaging essays from a wide spectrum of American Muslims writing about issues in their personal lives and communities.

DONNA LEE BOWEN and EVELYN A. EARLY (eds), *Everyday Life in the Muslim Middle East* (Bloomington: Indiana University Press, 1993)

A large number of short essays grouped thematically, which provide a window into Middle Eastern society.

RICHARD W. BULLIET, *Islam: The View from the Edge* (New York: Columbia University Press, 1994)

A scholarly but readable book that tries to show the importance of what are often considered societies peripheral to the development of Islamic culture.

DAN COHN-SHERBOK (ed.), *Islam in a World of Diverse Faiths* (New York: St. Martin's Press, 1991; rpt. 1997)

A scholarly set of essays by Muslim, Christian, and Jewish writers exploring the impact of Islam on pluralistic society.

KENNETH CRAGG and MARSTON SPEIGHT, *Islam from Within: Anthology of a Religion* (Belmont, CA: Wadsworth, 1980)

Written as a textbook, this is a good source of original Islamic texts dealing with a variety of subjects.

FARHAD DAFTARY, *The Isma'ilis: Their History and Doctrines* (Cambridge: Cambridge University Press, 1990)

A lengthy but engaging treatment of the Isma'ili Shi'i sect.

FREDERICK MATHEWSON DENNY, *An Introduction to Islam* (New York: Macmillan, 1994)

A well-organized introductory textbook, particularly strong in its treatment of Indonesian society.

KEVIN DWYER, *Arab Voices: The Human Rights Debate in the Middle East* (Berkeley: University of California Press, 1991)

A collection of essays that demonstrate the variety and complexity in the debate about human rights.

E. VAN DONZEL (ed.), *Islamic Desk Reference: compiled from the Encyclopaedia of Islam* (Leiden: E.J. Brill, 1994)

A short, useful book, providing easy-to-find information on Islam.

ASGHAR ALI ENGINEER, *Islam and Liberation Theology: Essays on Liberative Elements in Islam* (New Delhi: Sterling Publishers, 1990)

The author focuses on a narrowly Indian context, but provides useful arguments in favor of seeing some Islamic social movements as part of a worldwide movement of liberation.

CARL ERNST, *The Shambala Guide to Sufism* (Boston: Shambala, 1997)

An informative, thorough, and highly readable introduction to Islamic mysticism and its place in society.

JOHN L. ESPOSITO, *Islam: The Straight Path*. 3rd edn (New York and Oxford: Oxford University Press, 1998)

A popular introductory treatment of Islam, particularly strong in its treatment of the modern era.

JOHN L. ESPOSITO and JOHN Q. VOLL, *Islam and Democracy* (New York and Oxford: Oxford University Press, 1996)

A clear treatment of issues facing Muslim political societies in a number of contexts.

RICHARD ETTINGHAUSEN and OLEG GRABAR, *The Art and Architecture of Islam, 650–1250* (New York: Viking Penguin, 1987)

An excellent overview of the subject by two of the most respected authorities in the field.

ABU HAMID AL-GHAZALI, *The Ninety-Nine Beautiful Names of God: al-Maqsad al-asna fi sharh asma Allah al-husna*. Trans. David B. Burrell and Nazih Daher (Cambridge: Islamic Texts Society, 1995)

An enchanting meditation on the nature of God by one of the most widely read medieval Muslim theologians and mystics.

ABU HAMID AL-GHAZALI, *The Remembrance of Death and the Afterlife: Kitab dhikr al-mawt wa-ma ba'dahu*. Trans. T.J. Winter (Cambridge: Islamic Texts Society, 1989)

A fascinating overview of medieval attitudes toward death, written by one of the most widely read medieval Muslim theologians and mystics.

MEHRDAD HAGHAYEGHI, *Islam and Politics in Central Asia* (New York: St. Martin's Press, 1995)

A scholarly survey work on an important part of the Islamic world that has, until recently, been largely cut off from the course of world events.

MARSHALL G.S. HODGSON, *The Venture of Islam*. 3 vols (Chicago: University of Chicago Press, 1974)

An exhaustive and authoritative treatment of the central Islamic lands from the advent of Islam until the twentieth century.

STEPHEN R. HUMPHRIES, *Islamic History: A Framework for Inquiry* (Minneapolis: Bibliotheca Islamica, 1988)

A scholarly but very readable discussion of how best to understand the course of Islamic history.

SHIREEN HUNTER, *Iran after Khomeini* (New York: Praeger, 1992)

An informative book on Iran after the death of Ayatollah Khomeini.

ROBERT IRWIN, *Islamic Art in Context* (New York: Harry N. Abrams, 1997)
A beautifully illustrated and very engaging attempt to show the relationship between Islamic art and society.

G.H.A. JUYNBOLL, *Muslim Tradition: Studies in Chronology, Provenance, and Authorship of Early Hadith* (Cambridge: Cambridge University Press, 1983)
A learned, analytical treatment of the history and nature of Hadith.

GILLES KEPEL, *The Prophet and Pharaoh: Muslim Extremism in Egypt*. Trans. Jon Rothschild (London: Al Saqi Books, 1985)
Focusing on the groups that assassinated former Egyptian President Anwar Sadat, the book demonstrates how the ideas of Islamist writers have been adopted by extremist political groups.

MAJID KHADDURI, *The Islamic Conception of Justice* (Baltimore: The Johns Hopkins University Press, 1984)
An important work on aspects of Islamic ethics.

ROBERT D. LEE, *Overcoming Tradition and Modernity: The Search for Islamic Authenticity* (Boulder: Westview Press, 1997)
A scholarly but clear treatment of critical aspects of the religious thought of four important twentieth-century Muslim thinkers.

PHILIP LEWIS, *Islamic Britain: Religion, Politics and Identity among British Muslims* (London: I.B. Taurus and Co., 1994)
A comprehensive treatment of issues involving the Muslim community in Great Britain.

RICHARD C. MARTIN, *Islamic Studies: A History of Religions Approach*. 2nd edn (Upper Saddle River, NJ: Prentice Hall, 1996)
A good introduction to Islam that goes beyond simply outlining Muslim beliefs and practices to situate itself within the wider field of the historical study of religion.

N. I. MATAR, *Islam for Beginners* (New York: Writers and Readers Publishing, 1992)
An interesting introduction to important aspects of the religion, making extensive use of graphics.

AMINAH BEVERLY MCCLOUD, *African American Islam* (New York and London: Routledge, 1995)
The most comprehensive overview of the subject.

FATIMA MERNISSI, *The Veil and the Male Elite: A Feminist Interpretation of Women's Rights in Islam*. Trans. Mary Jo Lakeland (Reading, Massachusetts: Addison-Wesley, 1991)
An important book that argues for a feminist reexamination of the early sources of Islamic religious history.

MOOJAN MOMEN, *An Introduction to Shi'i Islam* (New Haven: Yale University Press, 1985)
A lengthy but clear and well-organized introduction to the subject.

SACHIKO MURATA and WILLIAM C. CHITTICK, *The Vision of Islam* (New York: Paragon House, 1994)
A fine introduction to Islam intended for the dedicated reader who is primarily interested in the spiritual aspects of the religion.

H.T. NORRIS, *Islam in the Balkans: Religion and Society between Europe and the Arab World* (Columbia: University of South Carolina Press, 1993)
The most comprehensive book on the subject.

FAZLUR RAHMAN, *Islam*. 2nd edn (Chicago: University of Chicago Press, 1979)
A widely read introduction to Islam written by a respected Muslim scholar.

FAZLUR RAHMAN, *Major Themes of the Qur'an* (Minneapolis: Bibliotheca Islamica, 1980; rpt. 1989)
A clear yet scholarly book that attempts to present the author's extensive reflections on the Qur'an

to a nonspecialist audience.

A. KEVIN REINHART, *Before Revelation: The Boundaries of Muslim Moral Thought* (Albany: State University of New York Press, 1995)
An important scholarly book on questions of morality and ethics.

JOHN RENARD, *Seven Doors to Islam: Spirituality and the Religious Life of Muslims* (Berkeley: University of California Press, 1996)
An excellent and highly recommended introduction to Islam, providing the variety and richness of the religion and the cultures with which it is affiliated.

JOHN RENARD (ed.), *Windows on the House of Islam: Muslim Sources on Spirituality and Religious Life* (Berkeley: University of California Press, 1998)
The best anthology of translated materials from a wide range of contexts.

YANN RICHARD, *Shi'ite Islam*. Trans. Antonia Nevill (Oxford: Blackwell, 1995)
A clearly written, scholarly work on the subject.

ANDREW RIPPIN and JAN KNAPPERT (eds), *Textual Sources for the Study of Islam* (Chicago: University of Chicago Press, 1986; rpt. 1990)
An excellent collection of translated materials from a wide range of contexts, all thematically arranged.

JOHN RUEDY (ed.), *Islamism and Secularism in North Africa* (New York: St. Martin's Press, 1994)
A scholarly but accessible introduction to the subject.

MALISE RUTHVEN, *Islam: A Very Short Introduction* (Oxford: Oxford University Press, 1997)
An extremely brief introduction that emphasizes the political aspects of the religion.

ANNEMARIE SCHIMMEL, *As Through a Veil: Mystical Poetry in Islam* (New York: Columbia University Press, 1982)
An engaging introduction to the nature and role of mystical poetry.

ANNEMARIE SCHIMMEL, *Mystical Dimensions of Islam* (Chapel Hill: University of North Carolina Press, 1975)
A very engaging introduction to Sufism by one of the most respected scholars in the field.

MICHAEL SELLS (trans. and ed.), *Early Islamic Mysticism: Sufi, Qur'an, Mi'raj, Poetic and Theological Writings* (Mahwah, New York: Paulist Press, 1995)
A collection of well-selected readings, exquisitely translated.

MUHAMMAD ZUBAYR SIDDIQI, *Hadith Literature: Its Origin, Development and Special Features*. Edited and revised by Abdal Hakim Murad (Cambridge: Islamic Texts Society, 1961; revised ed. 1993)
A very scholarly, but valuable overview of the subject of Hadith written from a traditional Muslim perspective.

BARBARA F. STOWASSER, *Women in the Qur'an: Traditions and Interpretation* (New York: Oxford University Press, 1994)
An important, exhaustive treatment of the subject.

RICHARD TAPPER (ed.), *Islam in Modern Turkey: Religion, Politics and Literature in a Secular State* (London: I.B. Tauris and Co., 1994)
A fine introduction to the subject.

B. TIBI, *Islam and the Cultural Accommodation of Social Change*. Trans. Clare Krojzl (Boulder: Westview Press, 1991)
An important scholarly treatment of some of the problems facing Islamic society in the contemporary world.

Internet Resources

Websites are somewhat ephemeral by nature. The following list of useful Internet addresses was accurate at the time when this book went to press.

http://goon.stg.brown.edu/quran_browser Qur'an Browser. A searchable database of the Qur'an, with a choice of translations by M. M. Pickthall, Abdullah Yusufali, and M. H. Shakir.

http://homepages.iol.ie/~afifi Maintained by the Belfast Islamic Centre. A news service, extensive links, sermons, and answers to questions by Shaykh Sayyid Mutawalli al-Darsh of Al-Azhar University, Cairo, and Chairman of the U.K. Shari'a Council.

http://www.ais.org/~islam The Islamic Interlink. Searchable information geared toward Muslims and individuals interested in converting to Islam.

http://www.arches.uga.edu/~godlas An informative website with information on educational opportunities in the Islamic world and a wide range of other Islamic topics. It is especially strong on Sufism and art. Maintained by Professor Alan Godlas, University of Georgia.

http://www.cais.com/islamic/home.html World Assembly of Muslim Youth's IslamNet. A valuable site with links to Qur'an, Hadith, and Fiqh databases, news and discussion groups, as well as to online books, articles, and other Islamic organizations. The "Fatwa System" provides a sophisticated input system to search previous *fatwas* and request new ones (low graphics).

http://www.epix.net/~sarieh A sophisticated website with extensive, searchable information and services for Muslim adults and children, artwork, chat groups, a matrimonial advertisement section, and an introductory page for non-Muslims. Several links to services providing *fatwas* and maintaining databases of *fatwas* that have already been issued.

http://www.icna.com/main.shtml A sophisticated website belonging to the Islamic Circle of North America, a large organization serving the needs of the Muslim community. A large variety of resources including a news service, chat rooms, a children's section, and a "Ladies' Wing."

http://www.islamicity.org/DEFAULT.htm Islamicity. A searchable site emphasizing commercial and educational information as well as matrimonial advertisements.

http://www.mds.qmw.ac.uk/student/islamic Maintained by the Islamic Society of St. Bartholomew's and the Royal London School of Medicine and Dentistry. A variety of information geared primarily towards Muslims. Notable for its discussion of medical ethics (supports frames).

http://www.princeton.edu/~humcomp/alkhaz.html Al-Khazina: The Treasury. Educational website with information and links concerning the Qur'an, searchable Hadith databases, a historical chart, many maps and photographs. Link to a Hajj site with

images and detailed information on the Hajj
(http://www.princeton.edu/~humcomp/vhajj.html). Maintained by Professor
Jerome W. Clinton, Princeton University.

http://www.qss.org An informative and well-maintained site run by the al-Qur'an was-
Sunnah Society. Extensive information geared toward Muslim adults and children.
Information on summer camps run by the QSS.

http://www.salaam.co.uk/main.html Sala@m. A clearinghouse for information with a
good search engine. The best links for Islamic services, mosques, and events in the
U.K.

Index

Page numbers in *italics* refer to picture captions.

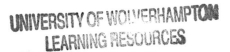